Your Employers' Profits

First published 1975 by
Pluto Press Limited
Unit 10, Spencer Court, 7 Chalcot Road,
London NW1 8LH

Copyright © Pluto Press, 1975

ISBN 0 902818 92 9

Printed by C. Nicholls & Company Ltd
The Philips Park Press, Manchester

Designed by Richard Hollis, GrR

Workers' Handbook No. 2

# Your Employers' Profits

Christopher Hird

Pluto Press

**Acknowledgements:**

Although everything that appears in this book is my own responsibility, many people have helped me with it.

I am grateful to Dorothy Morris and Howard Harrison for answering my many queries about the finer points of accountancy.

John Harrison, Alan Watts, Alastair Hatchett, Pat Kinnersly and Bob Ebsworth read the manuscript and commented on it. I have incorporated many of the valuable suggestions they made.

I am grateful to Richard Hollis for designing the book. My greatest debt is to Mike Kidron who has given me unending help and encouragement. Without him the book would never have appeared.

# Preface

In the summer of 1972 British companies were announcing big profit increases and expecting more in 1973. The *Financial Times* share price index reached record heights at over 500. Most of this book was written against this background. The *Financial Times* Index is now lower and British companies have suffered a profit collapse.

The companies and the government are taking this collapse seriously. Workers also need to, but not for the same reasons. They should remember:

First, although profits have tumbled, the surplus of which they are only a part, has not dropped nearly as much. Trading companies have simply transferred more of their share of the surplus to the banks and to the government. For workers the real target is the total surplus they produce, not only that part of it which happens to be called profits.

Second, the severity of British capitalism's crisis is partly of its own making. When companies were making huge profit's, they squandered them. Between 1970 and 1973 annual profits of British industry rose from £9,614 million to £17,035 million, making a total over the period of £40,407 million. We can see what the system as a whole did with this by looking at who borrowed money from the banks. Between 1970 and November 1973 bank lending to manufacturing industry increased from £3,512 million to £6,658 million, whilst lending to property companies rocketed from £336 million to £2,321 million and lending to other financial institutions – much of which went into property – increased more than five times to £2,737 million. British companies are short of cash now because the surplus of the boom years was squandered on such unproductive activities. There is no reason why workers should pay for this.

This book is a handbook. Companies will continue to produce Reports and Accounts and these will be the main source of information about companies. The explanations in this book of how accounts work and what terms mean apply whether profits be high or low. This year more workers than ever before will be told their employer faces bankruptcy. Some of these claims will be true; some will be false. Workers need to know the truth because it determines the tactics they will use to defend their jobs and wages. I hope this book will help them.

January 1975

# Contents:

# Part Two:

# Introduction:

Workers are used to being told that their employers can't afford to pay more wages, that the company is on the verge of bankruptcy and that profits are necessary to provide more jobs and better products.

Special sets of accounts for employees are produced to reinforce this propaganda. The truth of these claims can be checked by using the accounts that companies produce for shareholders. But even in these it is not possible to find every piece of information that is important – very few companies tell their shareholders how much they have to pay in rent, for instance.

The information is often disguised or hidden. It has to be searched for. The purpose of this book is to help workers do just that.

There are two big advantages to understanding company accounts:

1. It is the way to find the size of the surplus produced by the workers.

2. It provides some of the information needed to argue with management claims.

It is important to know if the company really is near bankruptcy, when pressing a claim. The tactics for ensuring better wages and a continuation of jobs depend on that knowledge.

There is nothing mysterious or magical about understanding company accounts or knowing where to find financial information.

Anyone can do it and this book should be some help.

# How to use this book:

**Workers need to know:**

■ What they can get in any bargaining situation.

■ Where the money will come from.

■ How secure they are in bargaining – is the company really going bankrupt? How important is a particular part of the company to any group of workers?

**To achieve this workers need to discover:**

■ Who controls and owns the factory and firm

■ The size of the firm's surplus.

■ The size of the firm's true profits and how they appear in its accounts.

■ The firm's plans for the future.

**This book is a handbook to help discover this information so that the worker can get a bigger share of the social product.** It is a handbook to the main sources of information about companies, especially their **Report and Accounts**. It is a handbook to help workers understand what is going on; to help them get hold of the surplus they produce. But because it is a handbook, it should not be read from beginning to end. The diagram on page 12 shows you how to start.

Although the book is mainly concerned with wealth in private industry, much of it is applicable to nationalized industries. Their accounts are presented in a very similar form and their success is measured in the same way: by the level of profitability. They use the same techniques to maximize the wealth extracted from workers: increased productivity, expansion in low wage and badly unionized areas, threats of redundancy and attempts to establish a fake community of interest between the company – which wants to maximize profits – and the workers who produce that profit.

All companies are obliged by law to produce an annual Report and Accounts, which is a record of the company's profitability and wealth. These accounts are produced for shareholders, not workers or the taxman. They may disguise the level of real profits.

---

## How to use this book:

Start: → Read Chapter 1.
Do you work for
a limited liability
company?

No ↓    Yes→ Is it a public
company?

Is it a nation-
alized company? No ↓    Yes→ Get a copy of
the annual
See Chapter 3  ←Yes    ↓No  Is it a private    accounts
company?    (see Chapter 2:
Then read 4)
Is it a partner-
ship or an    No ↓    Yes→ See Chapters
individual?    4 and 6

Is it a subsidiary
See Chapter 1  ←Yes    ↓No  of a private
company?
Is it a local
authority?    No ↓    Yes→ See Chapter 5

See Chapter 3  ←Yes    ↓No  Is it a foreign
company or
Is it a charity?  owned by one?

See Chapter 3  ←Yes    ↓No  No ↓    Yes→ See Chapter 2
page 33
Start again  Start again

---

A director of a **public company** (see page 149) has problems: he will want to show the shareholders that the company has a high level of profits and that it is rich in assets. He will often want to show the unions and workforce that the company is not profitable and cannot afford to pay high wages. Most businessmen benefit personally from higher profits – by having a large shareholding in the company, having a profit-linked commission agreement, or knowing that their promotion depends on results. For this reason most of them will run the risk of not being able to fool the unions and the workers about financial statements.

In a **private company** (see page 151), where the managers and the shareholders are generally the same people, there is one overriding aim: to minimize payment to the taxman. There will thus be a tendency to show profits as low as possible. This attitude is sometimes present in public companies when they are controlled by one family or individual. The family will be as anxious to minimize payments to the taxman as a private company. They will feel their wealth and the company is more secure if it is conservatively valued.

Businessmen often favour secrecy because it keeps their competitors in the dark about their real profitability and it discourages public attention from being focused on the company.

■ *'We think the directors will be unable for much longer to defer showing the real profits that have already been made but not shown in the profit and loss account.'* – Stockbrokers Sandleson & Co, writing about Wimpey, in 1972.

Until 1972 Wimpey's chairman, Sir Godfrey Mitchell, and trusts established by him controlled over 55 per cent of the company's shares.

■ *'Currys have always maintained a conservative approach towards the statement of the annual profits figures.'* – Stockbrokers LaurieMilbank & Co in a circular, June 1972.

The directors of Currys control 19 per cent of the company's shares; six of them are members of the Curry family.

There are other implications of the conflict faced by directors of public companies: in some cases profits may be overstated – to increase the share price. The result is that the company is financially much less sound than it appears to be. It is as important for workers to realize when this is happening as when profits are being hidden or purposely understated. A company that appears to be very profitable may be on the verge of bankruptcy.

Generally shareholders are not very demanding – so long as there is a profit figure in the **Profit and Loss Account** they do not concern themselves unduly with how it was achieved. As a result the accounts do not provide a full record of how the profit figure is arrived at. Sometimes it is impossible to know what accounting techniques have been used. Information about profits is therefore ambiguous. But much of the information about their real size can be discovered. **This book uncovers some of the techniques businessmen use to disguise the size of their profits.** It shows how easy or difficult it is to isolate particular devices for understating or overstating profits. And it shows how to establish the real size of the surplus, using publicly available documents.

# Laporte's two stories:

In May 1974 the 5,000 UK employees of the chemical firm Laporte received a glossy report telling them what a good year it had been for their employers. This was a rather slimmer volume than the one sent to shareholders – the lucky recipients of £1.5million of dividends and eventual beneficiaries of the **£10 million surplus** produced for them by the workers. But any employee reading the report sent to him would find that the company made **profits of £7.4 million.**

This is not the only piece of information that might have misled him. **The employee accounts showed that the company spent £5.9 million on new plant and machinery. In fact it spent virtually nothing.** The employee accounts showed that the company paid tax of £3.6 million, when it actually paid £3.2 million.

There were also several gaps in the employee accounts. They didn't mention that twelve directors shared salaries of £140,000. Eight of the directors were particularly lucky because they were paid £130,000 of that total. The remaining four were 'non-executive'. That means their contribution to running the company was to turn up for the occasional board meeting.

There was no mention that for years the company had been spending money on expansion in areas such as Portugal, Spain, South Africa and Brazil.

**For this sort of information the worker would need the accounts sent to the shareholders.**

Laporte makes its profits from chemicals used in a wide range of goods, such as paints, washing powders and tyres.

The employee accounts dealt in some detail with the company's products and their uses. They also gave a list of the company's main factories in this country. **This information, which was not in the shareholders' accounts, can be used to co-ordinate company-wide action and blacking,**

But the company wasn't aiming to provide information that was of any real use to the workers. The purpose of the report sent to employees was to create a phoney identity of interest between the company and the worker. That is why the report began with a message from the Chairman, referring to 'our company'. **The Chairman is paid £15,000 a year, or £288 a week. The average UK wage in Laporte is £2,203 a year, or slightly over £40 a week.** Although it is true that the 5,000 employees of Laporte would be out of work if the company didn't exist, the main purpose of the company is not to provide them with work. Its main purpose is to produce profits for the owners.

It is likely that more and more companies will produce accounts for their employees. This is partly in response to demands for worker involvement in running industry and partly as a public relations exercise to persuade workers that profits are necessary for everyone's good.

But as no management wants its power over the work force seriously threatened and as the level of profits is often far higher than is necessary for the investment in machines that will provide jobs, these documents are likely to be misleading. Laporte's was no exception.

There are two main profit centres in Laporte: its own factories – mainly in the UK and Australia – and its 50 per cent share in a company called Interox. All the factories in Interox are abroad and this is the area in which Laporte have been concentrating most of their expansion in the last three years.

The accounts that Laporte sent to its employees showed a profit of £7.4 million. This was the profit before tax. The workers produced a surplus larger than that, but £1.4 million had been paid in interest payments – the share received by owners of money lent to the company.

The surplus was even greater than this. The trading profits (pretax + interest) of £8.8 million were arrived at after deducting depreciation. In the employees' accounts the £3.6 million of depreciation is described as 'for the renewal of plant, buildings, etc'. The shareholders' accounts show that the allowance was actually much higher than this and hardly any of it was spent on renewing plant and machinery.

The depreciation allowance was actually £4,051,000. That is the amount of money the company could deduct from its profits to cover the fall in value of machinery before being liable to tax. Although it deducts this sum from profits, to arrive at its tax liability, it still keeps the money in the business. However, since the company received £435,000 from the government in grants, it added this to pretax profits by reducing the depreciation figure.

In addition to the £3.6 million net depreciation, the employee accounts show that profits of £2.3 million were being kept in the business for 'investment in new plant and working capital'. The employee might think that this meant that the company was spending £5.9 million (£2.3 million + £3.6 million) on new investment. But the shareholders' accounts show that during the year the company spent only £2.3 million on new fixed assets. As it acquired something like £2.75 million from selling assets, net spending on new plant and equipment was nil. No mention of all this in the employees' accounts. No mention either of how much tax the company didn't pay. The employees' accounts show that £430,000 of this wasn't paid at all. The system of government incentives to companies meant that Laporte could keep the money – interest free – to pay at some date in the future.

The company is also rather reticent about how much tax its shareholders pay. The employee accounts show the company paid dividends of £1.5 million. It doesn't say that this is after shareholders have paid income tax of 33 per cent.

Nor do the employee accounts show that Laporte's investment in Interox has grown by 15 per cent since it was formed in 1971, though the investment in its own assets has fallen by 8 per cent. You need the shareholders' accounts to discover this. But just to reassure the workers that the benefits of Laporte's profits are widely spread, the accounts claim that 'approximately 65 per cent of dividends are paid to institutions such as insurance companies, trustee and investment and holding companies, pension funds and other corporate bodies and approximately 35 per cent of dividends are paid to individuals'. But the shareholders' accounts show that insurance companies and pension funds – the only institutions that ever begin to represent the savings of ordinary people – receive only 22 per cent of the dividends.

# Appledore, Kitson and the Prime Minister:

The search for the information to fight employers can also produce information that has valuable propaganda value.

In 1973 some shipbuilding workers in the North-East were anxious to discover the profits of a company called A. & P. Appledore International. This was not hard. The company's accounts were available at Companies' House (see page 27). They were instructive enough: the company made profits of £85,000, after paying its directors £35,500 and allowing them travelling and entertainment expenses of £7,600.

But much more interesting was the fact that one of the directors was Timothy Kitson, MP and private secretary to Edward Heath, who was Prime Minister. Kitson became a director of this company in June 1972 – well after he had become Heath's right-hand man. Apart from a large farm which he owns, this appears to be the only business interest Kitson has. It is particularly unusual that he should have taken up the job after he had accepted a senior political appointment – when most government ministers are (temporarily at least) giving up business interests.

A. & P. Appledore advise on the building of shipyards. The company was owned by two ship and shipyard builders – Court Line and Austin & Pickersgill. Workers at the Savoy Hotel remember a lunch held there where the guests included several shipping magnates, Timothy Kitson and his boss, Edward Heath. No firm could have hoped for a better salesman for its skills than the Prime Minister himself.

But the generosity of the Tory government didn't stop there. One of the contracts on which A. & P. Appledore was advising was the building of Court Lines' Pallion yard on Wearside. Court Line, of course, owned part of A. & P. Appledore. The shipyard was to cost £10 million. Very conveniently the government agreed to lend the company the money to build the yard and also agreed that the rate of interest on the loan would be about half the commercial rate and no interest would have to be paid in the first two years.

Those with good eyesight and memory will remember that during the General Election in February 1974, Edward Heath was frequently seen getting off aeroplanes owned by Court Line.

This story would never have been uncovered if a group of workers hadn't been interested in the profits one company was making. But – more important – there were two reasons why it was possible to piece all the bits of the story together: A small understanding of the way in which the finances of companies work, and where the information is. And the existence of contacts between workers in different parts of the country through their own organizations.

Although the bosses and government may have a monopoly of information, they do not have a monopoly of skills.

To repeat: there is nothing mysterious or magical about understanding company accounts, or knowing where to find financial information. Anyone can do it and this book should be some help.

# Profits and surplus:

This book is about profits and it is about the surplus that workers produce for the owners of companies. They are not the same thing.

The profit a firm makes is often less than the surplus produced by the workers in that firm, because part of that surplus is appropriated by other firms or by government or by landlords. On the other hand profits sometimes include items that are not part of the surplus, like proceeds from the sale of property.

The distinction between surplus and profit is important for workers.

■ Only part of the surplus is available in any bargaining situation with a firm's management.

■ A company can be successfully producing goods and covering its costs, so there is a surplus. But the company may still be unprofitable and have to close down.

Workers are interested in both surplus and profit. Surplus is a measure of what the capitalist system as a whole takes from the workforce, profit is a measure of the share of surplus any particular company receives.

The importance of this distinction can be illustrated by the case of British Steel Construction, a company which has been running at a loss for several years. As the table below shows, in each year all the surplus has been appropriated by the bank and loan-stock holders, in the form of interest payments:

**British Steel Construction 1969–1973**

|      | Profit before interest £thousands | Interest paid | Pretax loss £thousands |
|------|------|------|------|
| 1969 | 318 | 1157 | 839 |
| 1970 | 504 | 1049 | 545 |
| 1971 | −540 | 1118 | 1658 |
| 1972 | −113 | 919 | 1032 |
| 1973 | 201 | 900 | 699 |

The company is clearly unprofitable and if things go on like this for much longer it will be bankrupt. But the workers still produced a surplus in three of the five years.

The distinction is particularly important in the case of nationalized industries, where the whole of the surplus often leaves the company.

It is important to know the size of the surplus when management says that a firm is unprofitable and there will have to be redundancies.

If there is a surplus, *the system as a whole* is capable of keeping the firm open. A company where there is no surplus at all is unlikely to survive under any economic system, but it is only under capitalism that companies need to be profitable. If there is no surplus at all (i.e. revenue does not cover costs) then the only way in which the company can improve its position is by increasing prices, reducing costs or receiving a subsidy from some other organization, like the state. But generally when companies start increasing prices, or cutting back jobs, it is not to ensure that suppliers are paid, it is to increase profitability – so that after the bank has been paid there is more left over, for the shareholders.

If workers are successful in fighting redundancies or increasing their wages in companies that are unprofitable, they will probably push the company nearer to bankruptcy. This should not necessarily discourage them. If a company is bankrupt it generally means that it can't pay the bank. It doesn't mean that it can't produce its products and pay its bills from the proceeds of selling them. It doesn't mean that the workers should be discouraged from struggling for that surplus. It simply means that their targets need to include all recipients of surplus, not only their immediate employer. It means that their tactics may need to be different.

**This book shows you how to find the size of the surplus. It also shows you how to find the size of the profits and shows ways in which they can be understated and overstated.**

Profits are not always part of the surplus. If a company receives grants from the government, it treats them as profits, but they are not produced by that firm's work force. If a company makes a profit on the sale of land, that profit is not part of the surplus produced by that work force. What is true is that the government's money originally came from that part of wages and profits that the government takes in taxes. The profit on land would not be possible without the original money used to buy the land – money that is part of the surplus. Nor would it be possible without the existence of the whole society around it which gives it its value. Nor could it be bought if the money that is used to buy it had not been made by workers somewhere in the economy.

The fact that profits are not always part of the surplus produced by the labour force in a company need not discourage workers from bargaining for it. But it is important to realize where profits are coming from: because it affects job security and helps to forecast whether those profits are likely to be there in the future.

Workers may want to negotiate over profits that are not part of the surplus they have produced or they may want to negotiate over parts of the surplus that are appropriated by other companies. It is important to realize what you are negotiating for because some parts of the surplus are more accessible than others and the tactics to be employed will be different.

# Checklist:

The information about a company's profits appears in different ways for different types of companies, so –

**First:**
Establish what type of company you work for. Chapter 1 explains how to do this.

**Second:**
Establish who owns the company for which you work. Chapter 2 will tell you how to do this.

**Third:**
Get hold of a copy of the company's annual Report. Chapter 2 will tell you how to do this.

**Fourth:**
Now you can start using the information in the accounts. The diagram on page 12 shows you how to find the chapter relevant to your particular employer. Each of the chapters will tell you how to discover the annual profits of the company.

You may want to know other things about the company:

- Is it going bankrupt?
- Is it liable to be taken over by an asset-stripper?
- Has it been expanding abroad?

Both the Glossary and the Index will guide you to the appropriate parts of the book to help you answer these questions.

If there are any terms you don't understand, use the Index to find out where they are explained.

# Part One:

## What to look for and —

## how to use what you find

# 1. The company you work for:

This chapter tells you how to find out what sort of enterprise you work for. The main possibilities are:

1. Limited liability companies:

a. public companies and their subsidiaries
b. subsidiaries of foreign companies
c. private companies

2. Partnerships

3. Nationalized industries and public corporations (e.g. the Post Office)

4. Local authority and government organizations (e.g. the Civil Service)

It is worth knowing the difference between these organizations and why businessmen choose one structure rather than another. This chapter and Chapter 2 deal with companies, Chapter 3 with other employers.

Chapter 12 explains the limited liability company, the difference between private and public companies and the various advantages and disadvantages of the different forms of a company. Most employees in the private sector – i.e. those not employed by the government, local authorities or nationalized industries – work for limited liability companies, so it is worth reading this chapter. (No figures are published showing a breakdown of the work force by corporate status of employer. However, using individual company figures, it can be estimated that 70 per cent of the work force in the UK works in private industry. Of this figure probably 90 per cent are employed by limited liability companies and at least 66 per cent by public companies, all of which are limited companies.)

# Limited liability companies:

**Is the company a limited liability company?**

The law requires all limited companies to use the word Limited (Ltd.) after their name in all official correspondence. Get hold of a piece of the firm's writing paper; look on the board outside the factory; get hold of an invoice or a receipt.

The law also requires the firm to print its registration number on official publications. This may be useful; look for it. Be sure to get the exact name of the company: with over a million companies, small mistakes can cause you a lot of trouble.

Although a company may call itself 'The Walls Meat Company' or 'The International Capitalist Conspiracy Limited', the law does not allow any official company name to begin with 'The'. So ignore any 'The' when looking up the company in any official reference work or in Companies House.

# Public and private companies:

**Who owns the company?**
**Is it a private or public company?**
**Why this is important.**

*It is important to know who owns the company you work for, so that you can assess the total wealth and power of the firm and discover where the surplus is hidden.* To discover this it is important to establish whether the firm is a private company or part of a public company. The terms 'public company' and 'private company' are explained in Chapter 12.

If it is a private company it may represent only part of an individual's wealth: profits being produced by the workers of one company may be transferred to another company owned by the same individual. If it is a public company all the profits are likely to be concentrated in that company.

But in a public company profits may be distributed around different parts of the group, at the directors' whim. It makes

# How to establish if you work for a private or public company:

**Start:**

→ Look in *Who owns Whom.* Is it there?
Yes ↓    No→

Is it a foreign company?
←Yes    ↓No

See if it is covered by any of the foreign services of Extel. (See Chapter 2) If not, look up your company at Companies House. See below ↓

Try *Kompass Directory* – is the ownership given there?
Yes ↓    No→

Look up parent company in *Stock Exchange Year-Book.* Is it there?
←No    ↓Yes

Is it public?
Yes ↓    No→

Then it is a public company. Read Chapter 2 on how to research it.

Try *Britain's Top 1000 Private Companies 1974/5* Is it there?
Yes ↓    No→

Then it is a public company. Read Chapter 2 on how to research it.

Then it's private. See Chapter 6.

You will have to try Companies House. See below.

Check on Extel or Moodies cards. If no luck, visit Companies House. See below. →

who owns the company and whether it is private or not. The information in Companies House is publicly available, so you could ask your employer who owns the company, is it private or not. He may tell you. But asking him may alert him to your interest.

## Companies House:

55 City Road, London EC1. This is where all companies have to register. There is a file for each company that includes the annual report, list of directors and list of share-holders. These files can be inspected by the public on payment of 5p each. If you don't live in London, ask a friend, your union or, as a last resort, one of the commercial organizations that carry out searches (such as Extel). You can soon tell from the file

no difference to the shareholders, so long as the profits are there in the end. By concentrating on the profits of the whole group, a real idea of the size of the surplus can be established.

Private companies are generally controlled by a small number of individuals, whereas public companies have hundreds or thousands of shareholders.

In a public company it is the directors' job to make profits for these shareholders. A private company has only a few shareholders, who will often be the directors. Profits can be hidden in another company – e.g. by using a discriminatory pricing structure (see page 63) and no-one will complain.

It is often difficult to establish the wealth of the owners of private companies. If a public company has a lot of subsidiaries, all the shares in those subsidiaries will be owned by the parent or holding company, (explained on page 178) so the size of the group's profits can be easily established. This is not the case with a private company. If you look at the list of shareholders of a private company, and it is just a list of individuals, do not assume that all their wealth is in that one company: they may own others. If they do they will be willing to shuffle profits from company to company, because although it won't make them any poorer, it may fool the workers or the taxman.

**But: directors of companies are meant to file at Companies House a full list of their directorships. Consult this and then, if you have time, look up all the companies of which they are directors.**

But the owners of private companies can disguise their ownership, and therefore their wealth and size.

# Partnerships:

If you work for a partnership (see Chapter 12) information is scarce:

**There are no statutory requirements for partnerships to publish financial information.** The only requirement that may cover them is that they register business names.

Anyone who trades under a name other than his own must register the business name, the general nature of the business and the chief place of business, at Companies House. But that is all, and many partnerships are clearly not covered by this.

But remember: with the exception of solicitors, accountants, most stockbrokers and a few other professional companies, only the smallest of businesses are partnerships and many small businesses register as companies, to take advantage of the protection of limited liability. (See pages 150–53).

# Targets for bargaining:

If you work for part of a public company, the target for bargaining is the annual Report and Accounts of the parent company.

If you work for a private company and there is a parent company, the parent company is only the first target. After that the target is the wealth of the owners. This can sometimes be established from all the companies which they own.

The owners of a company need not necessarily be directors of that company. And their shares may be held by a nominee company (see Glossary).

■ The Vestey family is believed to be one of the richest families in Europe. There is not a single company containing their worldwide business interests. Several members of the family are directors and owners of dozens of companies. One of the family's companies is called Midland Cold Storage. There are no Vesteys on the board, and the shares are held by Ulster Bank Nominees. In 1972 MCS tried to employ unregistered dock labour. The press and employers claimed it was a small company struggling to keep going, until the reality of its ownership was exposed.

To sum up: It is important to know whether your employer is a private company or part of a public company because the targets for bargaining differ, and the profit can be hidden in different places. In a public company, where the ownership is widely spread, the profit is likely to leave the company only by the payment of dividends.

Sometimes a public company is controlled by an individual or family that has other business interests. It is possible that the profits may be distributed from the public company to the private company. As the tax laws make this unattractive it is unlikely to happen but:

■ Movitex, a public company, rents its premises from a private company owned by the directors of Movitex.

■ CBR Jersey is a public company. It pays a private company owned by the directors and their family £40,125 a year for the rent of its head office.

This sort of distribution of profits from a public company to a private company, although rare, is important. It may represent a subsidy from the directors' private company to the public company. If the public company were to be taken over, this subsidy would stop and the new owners would be under greater pressure if they wanted to maintain the same level of profitability as in the past.

Money paid to the directors in this way is a more accessible target for bargaining than money which is paid to people unconnected with the company.

Profits are most likely to flow from private companies into public companies; if you work for a private company check if your employer has substantial interests in a public company. (An example of this is given on page 71 – Tompkins & Green Shield.)

# Useful sources:

How to find out whether the company is private or public:
There is no published list of companies which distinguishes between private and public companies. So use the chart on page 27.

Who Owns Whom:
Published annually by O.W.Roskill,
14 Great College Street, London SW1
Price £32 (July 1975)

This book is in two parts. In the first volume there is a list of all UK public companies, some major private companies, the major US companies operating in Britain and their subsidiaries. In the second volume there is a list of the subsidiaries of public companies, some major private companies and some US companies with the owning company listed opposite.

This is an invaluable book. It should be available in the reference section of any major library and in most major university or business school libraries. Ask your public library to stock the book and check with any student contacts if the book is available in their university or college library.

**Kompass Directory:**
More information about this on page 37, Chapter 2.

**Stock Exchange Year-Book:**
Published by Thomas Skinner & Co,
RAC House, Lansdowne Road, Croydon CR9 2HH
Price £15

This is a complete list of all quoted public companies.

It contains a list of their directors, the registered office, registrars, capital history and a summary of the last Balance Sheet.

The statistical information is not a great deal of help but the names and addresses of directors are useful.

**Extel or Moodies Statistical Cards:**

For information on these see page 34, Chapter 2.

**Britain's Top 1000 British Companies 1974/5:**

Graham/Trotman/Dudley Publishers Ltd.,
20 Souberts Place,
Regent Street, London W1
Price £9

This book lists the major private companies with brief details of profit and size.

# 2.

## Researching companies:

Is it a private company?

Yes ↓   No →   Then is it a public company? →

**Private company (Yes):**

What are its profits? (see left) →
- Use Extel Unquoted Service
- Go to Companies House

Who are its competitors? (see below)

Where are its factories? (see below)

Consult:
Kompass Directory
Dun and Bradstreet

**Public company:**

What are its profits? (see right) → Get a copy of its annual report

Where are its factories? (see below) → Use Moodies or Extel cards

Who are its competitors? (see below)? → Use Stock Exchange Circulars

Consult:
Kompass Directory
Dun and Bradstreet → To discover profits of its subsidiaries go to Companies House

# Researching companies:

If you have established whether you work for a private or public company (Chapter 1), this chapter tells you how to get hold of information which will help you find out the company's profits. See the diagram opposite.

Some of the sources will be useful in other ways too:
to discover possible suppliers – to organize blacking;
to discover the location of other factories in the same group of companies – to organize joint shop steward committees;
to discover competitors – to establish comparable wages.

# Annual Reports and Accounts:

These are obtainable from the company. The address of the company's head office will be in the *Stock Exchange Year-Book* or on the Extel card (see page 34). Most public companies will send you their most recent Report and Accounts free of charge on request. The Report and Accounts can also generally be obtained from the company's registrars.

### Private companies:
The Annual Accounts will be at Companies House.

### Foreign companies:
If you work for a company owned by a foreign company or for the foreign company directly, this is the procedure to follow:
1. Check if Extel cover the company in one of their foreign card services.
2. Go to Companies House to see the accounts of the particular company you work for.
3. Failing this, Standard and Poor's is an American statistical

service covering all American quoted companies. Very large businesses or public libraries may keep these. Or try a branch of one of the banks – although they won't have the service themselves, they could get it from a stockbroker.

**4.** If you still have no success, write to the head office of the foreign parent company asking for a Report and Accounts.

> ■ Ford, Chrysler (both American owned) and Philips (Dutch) all have registered subsidiaries in the UK, whose accounts are at Companies House. They are all covered in one of the Extel services.

**But:**

Concentrate on the accounts of the parent company because the companies may be shuffling profits from the UK subsidiary to an overseas subsidiary or the parent company. This can be done by intercompany pricing (see page 63).

### Extel or Moodies statistical cards:

These are two commercial organizations which tabulate the main financial information contained in the Report and Accounts, over a period of years. This is particularly useful in isolating the company's employment record.

Extel and Moodies cards are used extensively by stockbrokers, merchant banks and institutional investors (insurance companies and pension funds). Most national newspapers will subscribe to one of the services.

Ask anyone you know who works for this type of organization to help you. Many branch banks may have access to these cards.

Appendix 1 contains a list of libraries which subscribe to Extel Statistical Services, which is the easier one to understand. In addition to the service for UK quoted companies, there is a smaller service covering 1,000 unquoted companies and also a European and American service.

Extel sell individual cards on single companies – 50p each if it is a public company; £2 if it is in their unquoted service. Their address is:  Extel Statistical Services,
                                    37-45 Paul Street,
                                    London EC2A 4PB

There are other ways in which you might be able to get hold of this information:

### Pension funds:

About 12 million of the country's work force are members of a pension scheme, and the number is likely to increase. These schemes are 'funded' schemes. This means that the contributions are collected and put in a fund, which is invested on the worker's behalf. Some companies have their pension funds managed for them by a merchant bank. But some manage the funds themselves, often from the head office or main factory. They will have Extel cards, company Reports and Accounts and access to any information stockbrokers produce. Find out if your employer manages his own pension fund and if there is a specific department with responsibility for it. Try and make contacts in the department, directly or through the white-collar unions.

Pension funds have boards of trustees with responsibility for making sure the funds are managed properly. Workers should demand that they are (at least) represented on these boards of trustees. Use this representative to ask for any information you want.

### Stockbroking firms

Stockbroking firms operate in London and other major cities. They have large clerical staffs. Someone in your neighbourhood may well work there. Find out. Ask them to get information you want.

Use any journalists you know. Ask anyone who works in a bank to help – they have access to most statistical information available in the City.

### Remember:

Insurance companies, pension funds and banks keep stockbrokers in business. They will not hesitate to answer any enquiry from those organizations.

# Stock Exchange circulars:

These documents can be divided into three categories:

■ **Prospectuses:**

To obtain a quotation for their shares on the Stock Exchange companies have to produce a prospectus giving details about the company so that potential shareholders can judge the merits of the company. Although the information companies are required to provide is laid down in general terms, each prospectus has to be vetted by a department of the Stock Exchange, and as a result sometimes much more rigorous standards are applied than those laid down by the Companies Acts. Of course some public companies have been public for so long that it will be hard, if not impossible, to obtain the prospectus. The date on which the company became public should be in the *Stock Exchange Year-Book*, and will sometimes be on the Extel or Moodies card.

If the company has become a public company recently, the company, its registrars, merchant bank or stockbroker, may have a spare copy of the prospectus. The address of the first two can be obtained from the *Stock Exchange Year-Book* or Extel card, and the address of the second two will be on the abbreviated prospectus summarized on the Extel or Moodies card. As it is a requirement that all prospectuses be published in a newspaper, a copy of the *Financial Times* or *The Times* (and sometimes the *Guardian* or *Daily Telegraph*) will contain the prospectus at the time the company became quoted.

If the company obtained the quotation since the war, the reference source is the *Times Book of Prospectuses*, which, since 1970 has been called *Extel Book of New Issues of Public Companies*. Obtainable from Extel Statistical Services, 37/45 Paul Street, London EC2A 4PB. This book includes all prospectuses issued since the war. Although it is readily available in firms in the City, probably only the very largest public and university libraries will stock it.

■ **Quoted companies are required to produce circulars detailing any important acquisitions.** The amount of information varies with the size of the acquisition. Again copies of these can be obtained from the company or its registrars.

Whether any acquisitions have been made can be checked on the Extel card.

■ In any attempted takeover bid or merger, documents will be produced by both companies, which can be useful – particularly as they often contain promises (frequently broken) about future employment and forecasts of future profitability, and sometimes show shady deals by directors.

Some of these documents, as with the original prospectus, have to be filed at Companies House. Although the company's registrars or the merchant bank may keep back copies it will probably prove very difficult to obtain the documents if they are over a year old. However, they are easy enough to obtain at the time of the acquisition from the company's registrars, head office or bank.

# Reference books:

### Kompass Register of British Industry and Commerce:
Published annually by
Kompass Directories,
RAC House, Lansdowne Road,
Croydon CR9 2HH, in conjunction with
the Confederation of British Industries.

Volume I contains entries on almost 30,000 companies, many of them subsidiaries of public companies. The information provided is the name, address, bank, office hours, location, directors, share capital, product groups, number of employees. As the information is provided by the companies themselves there may be important gaps, but it is worth trying.

There is also a second volume which contains tables of product groups, showing which companies are manufacturers of these particular products. This is very detailed and can be very useful in discovering major competitors, possible suppliers and customers, to co-ordinate blacking or to establish comparative wage levels.

### Dun and Bradstreet's Guide to Key British Enterprises:
Published annually by Dun & Bradstreet,
PO Box 17, Adelaide House, London Bridge,
London EC4P 4AQ

This is a selection of approximately 11,000 of the most important firms engaged in manufacturing and distribution. The information provided may include reference to the parent company, factory locations, type of business, trade names, markets, number of employees, date of formation of the company and directors. A list of parent companies, showing their subsidiaries, and a classification of companies by business is also provided.

This book can be particularly useful in establishing the location of other factories or branches in a group.

### Dun and Bradstreet's Middle Market Directory:

This covers smaller, mainly private, companies in the same way.

### Kelly's Directory of Manufacturers and Merchants:

Annual. 150 firms are listed here alphabetically, with addresses, telephone numbers and products.

### Current British Directories:

Published annually by CBD Research, Beckenham, Kent.

This is a detailed list of both local and specialized trade directories with a subject index.

If any of these books are not available in the reference branch of your local library, request them, as they are invaluable.

### Directory of Directors:

Published by Thomas Skinner,
RAC House, Lansdowne Road,
Croydon CR9 2HH

A list of company directors and their directorships. This is by no means an exhaustive book, as the directors make their own entries, but it can be useful.

# Newspapers:

The activities of public quoted companies are newsworthy items because the ownership of the company is spread across the shareowning class. Newspapers are a useful source of information for reports of the profits and other important developments, interviews with directors, assessments of individual pieces of news, information about the general trading background of the industry in which the company operates.

The **Financial Times** is the most exhaustive. Many public libraries will keep back copies of the paper. The date on which profit figures are reported can be obtained from the Extel or Moodies cards.

The **Times** prints a yearly index to its contents and this makes looking through back copies much easier. Again major public libraries and university libraries are likely to keep back copies.

Some local libraries keep news cuttings of major companies or important local companies, e.g. Hull. So too do some university economics departments and most important, local newspapers. These places may also keep local companies' Reports and Accounts .

# Trade unions:

Some of the big trade unions – e.g. the AUEW – have research departments that will answer questions on companies and profits. But often they insist on the questions coming from a local official. The answers are not always sufficiently critical of the companies' own claims: the pretax profit figure is too readily accepted as the real profit.

Some unions claim they have no facility for answering such questions.

The power of the union's executive and central bureaucracy is partly based on having a monopoly of information. To give rank and file workers details of a company's profits may appear to threaten this power.

Ask your union to provide information about companies:

# Companies House:

See the diagram on page 27.

The accounts of private companies and the subsidiaries of public companies will appear rather different from the accounts of the public company. Chapter 4 explains how to understand a Profit and Loss Account. Chapters 5 and 6 explain the special features of the accounts of subsidiaries of public companies and of private companies.

# 3.

# Researching other employers

## The nationalized industries and public corporations:

**The biggest nationalized industries are:**

|                              | employees |
| ---------------------------- | --------- |
| The Post Office              | 416,400   |
| National Coal Board          | 353,900   |
| British Rail                 | 256,000   |
| British Steel Corporation    | 238,000   |
| Electricity Council          | 177,500   |
| British Gas Corporation      | 110,700   |
| National Bus Company         | 70,900    |
| National Freight Corporation | 52,000    |

Source: *Times 1000 1973–74*

The most useful sources of information about these companies are their annual Reports and Accounts, which are very similar to the accounts of private industry.

These can be obtained from Her Majesty's Stationery Office (HMSO) 49 High Holborn, London WC1V 6HB. They can also be ordered by post from the following branches:

PO Box No. 569, London SE1

Brazennose Street, Manchester M60 8AS

109 St. Mary Street, Cardiff CF1 1JW

13a Castle Street, Edinburgh EH2 3AR

258–259 Broad Street, Birmingham 1

50 Fairfax Street, Bristol BS1 3DE

7–11 Linehall Street, Belfast BT2 8AY

They like you to order from the nearest one. All HMSO publications are also available through booksellers, but where they are not individually stocked it will be as quick to order direct from HMSO. Large public libraries will probably stock the accounts of the largest nationalized companies.

Sometimes you have to pay for the annual accounts of the nationalized industries. Sometimes you can obtain the accounts direct from the industry's head office. This list shows the price and the addresses from which the reports can be obtained:

**Post Office**, HMSO. £1.50.
**National Coal Board**, Hobart House, Grosvenor Place, London SW1X 7AE, or HMSO. £1.50.
**British Rail**, British Railways Board, 222 Marylebone Road, London NW1 6JJ, or HMSO. £1.50.
**British Steel Corporation**, PO Box 403, Grosvenor Place, London SW1X 7JG. Free.
**Electricity Council**, 30 Millbank, London SW1P 4RD. Free.
**British Gas Corporation**, HMSO. £1.50.
**National Freight Corporation**, Argosy House, 215 Great Portland Street, London W1N 6BD. Free.
**National Bus Company**, 25 New Street Square, London EC4A 3AF. Free.

Chapter 7 tells you how to understand the accounts of the nationalized industries.

# Local authorities:

Local authorities have to produce accounts for the benefit of the ratepayers. They are published annually and can be viewed at the authorities' offices.

As local authorities do not have shareholders, any surplus left over at the end of the year is not called profit. But the annual accounts will show where the money comes from and where it is spent.

# Building societies:

Building societies have to produce annual accounts for their depositors. These are obtainable free of charge from the society's head office. Some branch offices keep a supply of them.

Building societies do not have shareholders in the same way that companies do and so the societies' profits are often not called profits:

■ Halifax Building Society 1972 accounts show 'Balance carried down: £7,778,002.' This is profit: it is what is left for the society after paying tax. It was added to the accumulated profits of £59,000,000 shown in the balance sheet. Total wages in 1972 amounted to £6.6 million.

# Charities:

All registered charities and friendly societies (which includes housing associations) have to produce accounts annually. Some of the larger organizations have a supply of them for public circulation, but they are all available from:

Registry of Friendly Societies, 17 North Audley St, London W1.

Charity Commissioners, 14 Ryder St, London SW1

# 4.

# The profits of a company

This chapter applies to **all companies, private, public or foreign-owned.** One exception: if you work for a merchant bank or a discount house, the Profit and Loss Account will not show the profits of the company. (See page 92).

The size of the surplus produced by the workers can be established from the **Profit and Loss Account,** by the following calculation:

**Pretax profits**
> PLUS **directors' fees**
> PLUS **interest**
> PLUS **part of depreciation** (sometimes)
> PLUS **exceptional items** (if any)
> PLUS **investment grants** (if applicable; see Chapter 14)
> PLUS **rent paid** (if given)
> PLUS **pension contributions** (if given)

This is the surplus; the profit from which higher wages can be paid is less. But, as explained on pages 18–20 above, much of the surplus goes in some form to other companies. This chapter (and Chapter 10) shows you how to do this calculation.

Chapter 2 showed how to find the accounts of a company. Chapter 3 dealt with employers other than those in private industry. Chapter 8 is a summary of what documents and information companies have to make available for public inspection, and Chapters 9, 10 and 11 list what has to be shown in the annual accounts. These chapters also explain the technical terms used in the accounts in the **Directors' Report,** the **Profit and Loss Account** and the **Balance Sheet.** Read these if problems arise, but first find the Profit and Loss Account in the annual Report and Accounts.

# Profit and Loss Accounts:

The Profit and Loss Account shows you the firm's profit for the last year. It will look like the diagram below. This shows that for the accounting period ending February 1973, the company made a profit of £12,120,000 before taxation.

**ENGLISH CALICO LIMITED**

## Group Profit and Loss Account
### for 53 weeks ended 3rd February 1973

|  |  | 1972/73 £,000 |  | 1971/72 £,000 |
|---|---|---|---|---|
| Sales |  | 182,948 |  | 162,919 |
| Trading profit before interest |  | 14,474 |  | 11,913 |
| Interest |  | 2,354 |  | 2,326 |
| Profit before taxation |  | 12,120 |  | 9,587 |
| Taxation |  | 5,665 |  | 4,567 |
| Profit after taxation |  | 6,455 |  | 5,020 |
| Minority Interests |  | 390 |  | 266 |
| Profit attributable to English Calico Limited |  | 6,065 |  | 4,754 |
| Dividends |  |  |  |  |
| Preference | 294 |  | 294 |  |
| Ordinary including Advance Corporation Tax | 3,594 | 3,888 | 3,423 | 3,717 |
| Profit retained |  | 2,177 |  | 1,037 |
| Earnings per ordinary share of 25p |  | 4·2p |  | 3·3p |

Profits of £1,132,000 (1971/72 £502,000) on sale of properties and investments have been credited to reserves. (Note 18).

Prior year tax adjustments less major reorganisation and closure costs after tax relief amounted to £124,000 which has been credited to reserves (1971/72 a credit of £41,000). (Note 18).

But this is not the size of the surplus that labour has produced. That amount, the real target for bargaining, is larger than the pretax profit figure.

To arrive at the real profit figure, various deductions made by the company need to be added to the pretax figure.

# Directors' pay:

This is generally called **Directors' Emoluments** and can usually be found in the Notes to the Accounts. Sometimes the money paid to the directors makes a substantial impact on profits.

> ■ In 1970 William Press Ltd made pretax profits of £2.11 million. This was after paying the nine directors a total of £303,247 in salaries: profits would have been almost 15 per cent higher but for this.
>
> £303,247 represents the wages of 155 William Press workers.

But:

Directors' fees may be an inadequate guide to how much the directors are paid. For more information on this see pages 71–2, 179.

# Interest payments:

This is interest paid on loans made to the company. It is paid to the owners of one type of capital – money which has been lent to the company.

The company is obliged to show what type of loans these are and how much is paid on each type (see page 126). Interest is paid to both the owners of loan stock and to the bank. This money is part of the surplus because it is being paid to one type of capital owner – the loan stock holder or the bank – in the same way that dividends are paid to the holders of ordinary shares.

There has been a trend over the last ten years towards financing the expansion of companies by loan capital and bank borrowings, rather than issuing more shares (see page 127). The result has been to reduce pretax profits in the early years of financing expansion.

But as the cost of this money is fixed, the owners of the ordinary shares benefit:

■ Companies increase profits by increasing sales, cutting costs and/or increasing prices. All the benefits of that increase go through to the ordinary shareholders because the loan stock holder receives a fixed sum in return for his loan.

■ In periods of inflation interest rates rise, so a company which has borrowed money several years ago is now borrowing more cheaply than the ruling rate of interest. In 1972 the average cost of long-term money to the 840 largest companies in the UK was 7.2 per cent. But when companies raised long-term finance that year, they had to pay over 10 per cent. Now (early 1975) they would have to pay over 15 per cent.

In the Profit and Loss Account shown on page 45, the interest payment amounts to £2,354,000.

The redistribution of the surplus between the owners of different types of capital (ordinary shares, loan stock and the banks) in no way reduces the total surplus created by labour. But the increasing importance of fixed interest borrowing, and therefore increasing interest charges, affects the profitability of *individual* companies. Money that companies used to have control over now goes to the bank, which is not represented at the wage-bargaining table.

### Management will claim:

*Interest has to be paid on loans as a cost of financing the business. Unless interest is paid it will be impossible to get finance needed to expand and so create job opportunities. These arguments aim to show an identity of interest between workers and the firm.*

### But the truth is:

The payment of interest is what the owners of capital receive for being fortunate enough to have had capital accumulated for them over the years. Only under capitalism do firms have to struggle with the cost of having to pay for resources that exist somewhere in society.

There is no guarantee that the expansion will be in the interests of the workers. There is no mechanism to ensure that any profits made from that expansion are even shared between the workers and the shareholders.

If management complain about the burden of interest payments, check what the dividend record has been over the years. Often the company is only borrowing because of a generous dividend policy.

The dividend record can be established from the Report and Accounts. Often companies produce a table showing the company's profit record over a period of time. The figures are also obtainable from an Extel or Moodies card.

■ In the year 1973, English Calico had total borrowings of £31 million. Since 1968 it had paid £17 million in dividends.

There is no reason why workers should sacrifice wages to pay interest on loans that are only necessary because profits have been given out in dividends.

But there is an important difference between the pretax profit and the pre-interest profit. It is easier to get hold of some of the pretax profit than the pre-interest profit. If a company cannot pay the interest on its loans, the results can be very serious (see pages 129–130). Interest payments are money that leaves the company and over which directors have little control. They have much greater control over what they do with pretax profits.

# Depreciation:

The machinery which companies buy falls in value as it gets older. Companies are allowed a tax-free deduction from profits to cover that fall in value. This deduction is called depreciation and is used to finance further investment.

Any society will need to accumulate a fund for the replacement of old machinery. But in some companies in our society the depreciation charge is greater than the amount needed to replace old machinery. This excess depreciation is another hidden profit and should be a target for bargaining.

When the depreciation figure exceeds spending on plant and machinery, the excess should be added to the pretax figure to establish the size of the real surplus.

**This is what to do:**
1. Find the depreciation figure – this will be in the Profit

and Loss Account or the Notes to the Account.

2. Find the value of any investment grants which have been added to after-tax profits: this is one way companies can make profits seem smaller than they actually are (see Chapter 14). Add any grants credited to after-tax profits to the depreciation figure.

3. Find out how much was spent on plant, machinery and buildings. This will be in one of the Notes to the Accounts which will show acquisitions and disposals of fixed assets, probably in the form of a table, as in the example on page 51.

4. Find out how much was received from the sale of plant and machinery. This can be established from the same table, but look under Reserves (page 123) and in the Profit and Loss Account to see if any of the plant was sold at a profit (above book value). If it was, count this surplus as part of the proceeds from the sale of plant and machinery.

Subtract 4 from 3. This will give you the net investment in plant and machinery.

If the value of the depreciation charge plus investment grants (1 plus 2) exceeds the net spending on plant and machinery (3 minus 4), the difference should be added to the pretax figure. An illustration of how to do this follows.

### How to establish net spending on plant and machinery:

Tables on page 51 show parts of ICI's 1973 accounts. They show how much the group and how much the parent company have spent on plant and machinery during the year. The worker is interested in how much the whole of the ICI group has spent: the top half of Table A.

The last column in the third line shows that the group spent £120 million. But line 4 shows that the company received £3.8 million from selling assets. This is the book value of the assets sold (i.e. the value of the assets after depreciation has been deducted from the cost). If any of the assets have been sold for a profit above the book value, this will be shown in the reserves figure. Table B shows the movement in reserves. ICI does not specify the exact profit made on the sale of assets, but it is included under the heading 'Other movements' on line 11: £5.9 million. There is no way of knowing how much of this is profit. Assume it all is – put the onus on management to disclose more information.

**Now you can establish the net spending:**
120.2 — (3.8+5.9) = 110.5 (in millions of pounds)
**But:**

Depreciation was £157.5 million – see line 5 in Table A showing changes in fixed assets. The company also had the benefit of investment grants to help it pay for plant and machinery. The value of these is shown in the Profit and Loss Account (see Table C). So, the value of government allowances is: 157.5 + 24.7 = £182.2 million.

**There is now sufficient information to complete the calculation:**

| | |
|---|---|
| Depreciation + investment grants: | 182.2 |
| Net spending on plant etc: | 110.5 |

| | |
|---|---|
| **Excess to be added to pretax profit** | **£71.7 million** |

Sometimes companies produce a **Sources and Uses of Funds** table, which shows how investment was financed. This will probably contain the information you need to establish the net investment figure.

■ Part of English Calico's Sources and Uses of Funds table is shown on page 53.
■ In 1972/73 the companies in the group spent £8.25 million on new plant and machinery. But they sold plant and machinery worth £5 million (including £1,132,000 profit over book value) and charged depreciation worth £4.9 million. So £1.7 million should be added to the pretax figure to establish real profits.

Even if a company seems to be spending more on investment than the depreciation charge, remember that this spending includes new investment and not just replacement. **This new investment may not be in the workers' interests:** it may be spent on machinery that will only create redundancies, or will produce goods that are unnecessary substitutes for those already being produced.

The depreciation charge may be especially high for two reasons: the company uses a system of depreciation that makes provision for inflation (see page 161) or the company

## Table A: I.C.I. Changes in assets

| Fixed assets | Land and buildings | | | Plant and equipment | | | Total |
|---|---|---|---|---|---|---|---|
| | Cost or as revalued £m | Depreciation £m | Net book value £m | Cost or as revalued £m | Depreciation £m | Net book value £m | Net book value £m |
| **Group** | | | | | | | |
| At beginning of year | 418·5 | 142·5 | 274·0 | 1,739·5 | 853·7 | 885·8 | 1,159·8 |
| Exchange adjustments | 26·0 | 6·5 | 20·5 | 69·7 | 32·0 | 37·7 | 58·2 |
| Capital expenditure | 19·4 | — | 19·4 | 100·8 | — | 100·8 | 120·2 |
| Disposals and other movements | 5·3 | 9·0 | 3·7 | 28·1 | 28·2 | ·1 | 3·8 |
| Depreciation for year | — | 17·6 | 17·6 | ·— | 139·9 | 139·9 | 157·5 |
| At end of year | 458·6 | 156·6 | 300·0 | 1,881·9 | 997·4 | 884·5 | 1,184·5 |
| **Company** | | | | | | | |
| At beginning of year | 181·4 | 79·7 | 101·7 | 1,179·2 | 587·0 | 592·2 | 693·9 |
| Capital expenditure | 5·5 | — | 5·5 | 60·4 | — | 60·4 | 85·9 |
| Disposals and transfers | 2·0 | 1·3 | ·1 | 26·1 | 24·6 | 1·5 | 1·6 |
| Depreciation for year | — | 8·4 | 8·4 | — | 90·4 | 90·4 | 98·8 |
| At end of year | 184·9 | 86·2 | 98·7 | 1,213·5 | 652·8 | 560·7 | 659·4 |

## Table B: I.C.I. Movement in reserves

**8 Retained profits and reserves**

Movements in Group reserves were:

| | Group 1972 £m | 1973 £m |
|---|---|---|
| Retained profit for the year — | | |
| by parent company | 10·8 | 61·5 |
| by subsidiaries | 8·9 | 60·9 |
| in associated companies | 4·6 | 11·3 |
| | 24·3 | 133·7 |
| Share premiums received | 6·8 | 3·7 |
| Amounts provided against investments | 4·6 | 1·6 |
| Goodwill written off — new subsidiaries | 4·8 | 3·9 |
| Revaluation of fixed assets | — | 4·2 |
| Exchange adjustments — | | |
| book value of overseas subsidiaries | — | |
| other | 1·6 | 29·1 |
| Other movements | 1·0 · | 5·9 |
| Total movements for year | 21·1 | 174·3 |
| At beginning of year | 448·6 | 469·7 |
| At end of year | 469·7 | 644·0 |

## Table C: I.C.I. Profit and loss account

| | | | | |
|---|---|---|---|---|
| Profit before taxation and grants | | 141·0 | | 311·0 |
| Taxation | | | | |
| ICI Group | 49·6 | | 215·5 | |
| Associated companies | 7·7 | | 14·7 | |
| | 67·3 | | 130·2 | |
| Less: Investment grants | 17·9 | | 17·9 | |
| | | 39·4 | | 112·3 |
| | | 101·6 | | 198·7 |
| Regional development grants | | 6·8 | | 9·2 |
| Profit after taxation and grants | | 108·4 | | 207·9 |

employs an exceptionally high rate of depreciation (see pages 160–61). Both these overstatements will be accounted for if you use the method described above in arriving at the real profit.

### Management will claim:

*Depreciation is an expense that is involved in running the business, almost like the electricity bill. Provision must be made for the fall in the value of the machinery, so that it can be replaced when necessary.*

### But:

Depreciation is not like the electricity bill: it is a tax-free allowance. **Depreciation is cash that remains in the company, in addition to retained profits, to be spent on plant and equipment.**

There is no dispute about the existence of depreciation, but about its size, its use and its control. Depreciation is often larger than that needed for replacement. It can be used to finance investment that is against the interests of the workers. The benefits go straight through to the shareholder.

Workers will not argue with the need to build a fund to replace old machinery. But the depreciation figure is often more than this, and it is a fund over which workers have no control.

Firms will also argue that profits are necessary to finance investment and so provide more jobs. In fact many companies can finance their investment from their depreciation allowance alone, so that even with very low pretax profits, investment plans are unaffected.

■ Page 56 shows how English Calico has financed all its expansion from depreciation and the sale of assets, paying dividends in 1969/70 even when the profits did not cover them. The labour force has fallen consistently.

When management starts complaining about needing money for future expansion:

### Find out:

■ How much has been paid out in dividends compared to how much has been spent on new fixed assets (capital expenditure).

**ENGLISH CALICO LIMITED**

# Source and Use of Group Funds

| Source | | 1972/73<br>£,000 |
|---|---:|---:|
| Profit attributable to English Calico Ltd. | 6,065 | |
| Increase in minority interests | 218 | |
| Prior year tax and other adjustments | 705 | |
| | | 6,988 |
| Tax equalisation | | 959 |
| Depreciation | | 4,914 |
| Sale of fixed assets | | 5,022 |
| | | 17,883 |

| Use | |
|---|---:|
| Expenditure on fixed assets | 8,254 |
| Increase in investments | 497 |
| Increase in working capital | 161 |
| Dividends | 3,888 |
| Decrease in loan capital and net short-term borrowings | 5,083 |
| | 17,883 |

■ How far capital expenditure is paid for by depreciation and retained profits.

*In 1972 the 840 major British companies spent £3,700 million on new industrial productive capital. Retained profits and depreciation amounted to £4,426 million. Investment grants amounted to £321 million.*

There is an important dispute about depreciation. Is the company making sufficient provision for the replacement of plant and machinery? If the company is not – then its profits are much lower than they appear and the firm is not as strong as it appears, so workers' job security is threatened. If it is, the company is stronger than many other companies showing similar profits but there is no way in which the worker can benefit from that increased financial strength.

Most companies calculate their depreciation on the basis of the original, or historic, cost of the machinery. When prices are rising rapidly the replacement cost will be much greater, so that the fund for replacement calculated on historic cost will be insufficient. If a company wants to replace machinery in the future, it needs more money than the original cost of the machinery.

Some companies prepare for this by establishing a special fund for replacement (see GKN example, page 161). They are introducing a system of accounting which makes allowance for this inflation in the cost of machinery, by showing company profits after making provision for the replacement cost. The effect of **inflation accounting** (see pages 105–109) is to reduce published profits.

But remember that the value of the company's existing machinery may rise in a period of high inflation as its second-hand value is determined partly by the cost of new machinery.

If a company does not make adequate provision to replace machinery, then it is overstating profits in the same way that a company which didn't make adequate provision for the payment of pensions it had promised, would be overstating profits. This can be dangerous for workers. Any worker who believed the accounts of Court Line in 1974 (as most did) would have been surprised when the company went broke at the cost of his job later that year (see pages 172–3 below).

The conflict for workers is obvious: if you accept management claims that a big reserve is needed to replace machinery, then you ensure a profitable and financially secure company. But there is no way in which you benefit from this. The price of any concession must be a share in future profits and the conflict can only be removed when companies are owned and controlled by the workers.

**Exceptional items:**

Some companies deduct non-recurring expenses – which are exceptional costs – *before* arriving at the pretax profit. To get an accurate idea of the size of the company's profits, these should be added to the pretax figure, as they are non-recurring and unrelated to the costs of production, although they might be a real cost. Remember the Profit and Loss Account is a historical record of the company's profits. The worker wants to establish the size of profits now. The Profit and Loss Account is useful when it helps to do this.

■ British and Commonwealth pretax profits in 1971 were £700,000 lower than normal because of the costs of promoting the tour and travel business for the next year's season.

■ Carrington Viyella's 1972 pretax profits were £735,000 lower because the company changed its depreciation policy.

Look for exceptional costs – they won't always be specifically called exceptional. Add them to the pretax figure. Read the Notes to the Accounts carefully: exceptional items are often hidden there.

Where the exceptional items have been deducted from or added to after-tax profits, normally they should be ignored because they have not distorted the pretax profit figure.

**But:**

Wimpey's 1970 accounts included an exceptional after-tax profit of £1.46 million. This was money the company had expected to lose on contracts but in fact didn't. When the provision for these losses was first made it was deducted from pretax profits. This means that pretax profits had been understated by this amount in the past.

**When an exceptional credit relates to normal trading activities rather than (for example) the sale of assets, add it to the pretax figure to arrive at the real surplus.**

**Pretax profit, plus interest paid, plus exceptional costs, plus (sometimes) part of the depreciation charge, is the surplus produced by the labour force, after the company has paid for labour, materials and overheads.**

## 56. Profits / Capital investment

In 1972/73 English Calico made a pretax profit of £12.12 million (see page 45). The company has 29,608 employees. So pretax profits per employee were £409. Adding in part of the depreciation, interest and directors' pay, surplus per employee equals £545.

### English Calico: some Sources and Uses of Funds

| Year ends 31 January | spending on fixed assets | sales of fixed assets | depreciation | addition to retained profits | no. of workers |
|---|---|---|---|---|---|
| | £ thousands | | | | |
| 1968/69 | 6807 | 2314 | 4637 | 1088 | 37,078 |
| 1969/70 | 7489 | 3725 | 4287 | —391 | 36,005 |
| 1970/71 | 6009 | 2315 | 4146 | 436 | 33,307 |
| 1971/72 | 7527 | 3105 | 4310 | 1037 | 32,317 |
| 1972/73 | 8254 | 5022 | 4914 | 2177 | 29,619 |
| 1973/74 | 10197 | 2168 | 5586 | 5827 | 29,244 |

Source: English Calico's Annual Accounts

**BUT the surplus may still be bigger than this.** So far it has been established by using information that must be shown in the accounts. But there are two more items that should be counted as part of the surplus produced by the workers. These are **rent** and **pension contributions.** Companies rarely show them. Rent is money paid to the owners of one type of capital: property. Pension contributions are money invested in a pension fund for the workers. In many companies the workers themselves make a contribution to the fund. But both the worker's and the employer's contribution is money produced by the workers, and pensions are only deferred pay.

There is no obligation on companies to show the amount of money paid in either rent or pension contributions. The Companies Acts, the Stock Exchange and the Institute of Accountants do not require it. But some companies show them and it seems likely that they will increasingly show the amount of money paid in pension contributions for reasons explained below.

# Rents:

Since the beginning of the 1960s there has been a substantial redistribution of the surplus within the company sector from manufacturing industry to property companies.

In 1961 British companies paid £160 million in rent. This represented 4.39 per cent of gross trading profits. In 1972 British companies paid £428 million in rent. This represented 7.4 per cent of gross trading profits.

This redistribution has probably been particularly marked in retailing, and some retailing companies show the amount of money they have paid in rent during the year:

> ◪ Even though W.H.Smith own a large number of their shops, rent paid in 1973/74 amounted to £1.672 million. This represents 17 per cent of pretax profits and £170 per W.H.Smith full-time worker.

**When the amount of rent paid is shown, it should be added to the pretax figure, to establish the size of the surplus. But money paid in rent is not the same sort of target for bargaining as the pretax profit: if companies didn't pay the rent, they would not be able to occupy their premises. In a capitalist economy it is** as important to pay rent as it is to pay the electricity bill. Rent, like interest payment, is a necessary transfer to the owners of one type of capital; companies must pay that money if they are to survive. But it is wealth produced by the workers nonetheless, and the company could produce goods just as easily without paying rent.

# Pensions:

Under the Labour government's Social Security Pensions Bill, all employees have to be members of an occupational pension scheme or of the state reserve scheme. As a result the number of workers who are members of pension schemes is likely to increase substantially. Barbara Castle, Labour's Minister of Health and Social Security, has said she approves of and wishes to encourage the establishment of occupational pension schemes, and the pension industry (insurance companies, merchant banks and various self-appointed experts) have conducted such a successful campaign that many managements, supported by the unions, will go ahead and introduce schemes.

In most cases this will mean that workers lose control over millions of pounds of their money, which will be invested in company shares and property. This is one reason why it is important for workers to know how much a company is spending on pensions and to know how highly companies value the security of the worker's pension.

This is how pension funds work: **During the worker's working life money is paid into a fund; this is invested and from the proceeds, the pension is paid when the worker retires.**

This is not the only way in which pensions could be provided. The major alternative is the establishment of a comprehensive state transferral scheme. Under this a fixed percentage of wages and profits would be transferred to the pensioners each year. Such a scheme would be simpler, fairer, more inflation-proof and no more expensive. However it would not serve the interests of British capitalism very well. So workers will have to cope with funded pension schemes for the time being.

The ways in which the money is collected for the fund vary considerably. Sometimes the company deducts a percentage of the workers' wages, and then makes up the rest of the contribution itself. Sometimes the company pays all the contribution. Sometimes the contributions are a fixed amount, sometimes they are a percentage of wages. But as all the company's money has been produced by the workers anyway, the workers effectively provide all the contributions.

The pension fund soon builds up to an enormous size, but it is controlled by the management or their appointees.

Because the pension fund guarantees the worker certain benefits it is important that the fund has enough money in it and is profitably invested. Actuaries are employed to make sure this is so, and funds which do not fulfill these requirements are actuarily unsound. This means the actuary has calculated that the fund is not big enough to pay the benefits promised.

As it is the company which guarantees the fund's benefits, a fund that is unsound or showing a deficiency is a contingent liability – it is money the company might have to pay under certain circumstances. It is possible that companies owe large sums of money that are not shown in their accounts.

There are a variety of ways in which companies can misuse pension funds. If the company just guarantees to 'top up' the workers' contribution, any surplus that is established in the fund can be used to reduce the employer's contribution rather than increasing the value of the benefits.

A company can delay the payment of contributions when it wants the money to finance expansion. This means the workers' pension fund is providing the company with an interest-free loan.

*'We believe the flow of money from company revenue into a pension fund should be integrated into the total operations of that company and play its role in helping the organization towards its final objectives.*

*'The only way that the employers' obligation can be reduced is through the return on investments.'*

From *Aggressiveness in Pension Fund Management*, published by the pension consultants, Pension Planners (Europe) Ltd.

To prevent this robbery workers need to know:

■ Whether their pensions are being paid from a fund which is actuarily sound or not.

■ Whether the employer is just topping up the workers' contribution.

■ Whether the employer is up to date with his contributions.

The only safeguard workers can have against management abuse of the pension fund is control of, or representation on, the fund's board of trustees.

■ In 1973 ICI showed pretax profits of £311 million. This was after pension fund contributions of £57.2 million. It included £20.0 million of special payment to a pension fund that was unfunded. That means that profits were £20 million lower because of an exceptional pension fund contribution. The £57.2 million is workers' money. They produced it and they will eventually benefit. But they have no control over it.

■ Ideal Standard is the UK subsidiary of American Standard of New York. The 1972 accounts show a trading profit of £1.7 million. But the company has a contingent liability of £531,000 in unfunded pensions. That means that over the years, instead of providing money for a fund to pay the pensions as was promised, Ideal Standard was using the money to finance expansions of the business.

Pension contributions are the workers' money. They are part of the surplus produced by the workers. The argument is not over the existence of pensions, but over the control of this money and how pensions are provided. Workers need to know the amount a company spends on pensions, because it helps establish the size of the real surplus and it shows if profits are exceptionally low; it helps establish the financial stability of the company.

**When the amount of money paid into a pension fund is shown, add this to the pretax profit figure.**

Management will claim that you are taking money away from the pensioners, by negotiating over contributions. This is not so. In most pension schemes there is no element of subsidy: a worker's own contributions provide a fund to pay that worker his pension. It is one of the major failings of the funded pension structure that those workers who are not fortunate enough to have been members of a pension scheme all their lives get a grossly inadequate pension.

**So, to repeat:**

**The surplus produced by labour** can be established by the following method:

**Pretax profits**

    PLUS **directors' fees**

    PLUS **interest paid**

    PLUS **part of depreciation** (sometimes)

    PLUS **exceptional items** (if any)

    PLUS **investment grants** (if applicable; see Chapter 14)

    PLUS **rent paid** (if given)

    PLUS **pension contributions** (if given).

This will enable you to establish the size of the surplus, but this is not the size of the company's real profits.

As explained on pp. 18–20 the rent and interest payment part of the surplus goes to other companies to make their profit. In a capitalist economy the company will go out of business if it cannot pay the rent or pay the bank. The firm's ability to pay higher wages is restricted by the amount of money it has to pay in rent and interest payments. Workers who want to recover that part of the surplus which has been taken in rents and interest payments need to bang on the doors of the property companies and banks.

The profits of an individual company must not be separated from those of industry and finance as a whole just because part of the surplus is redirected to other companies within the system. These companies are owned by the same class: a man with shares in a bank whose profits go up is not unduly concerned by a fall in profits in other companies in which he holds shares because of higher interest payments made to that bank. Ultimately the workers are struggling not just with their employers but with the system as a whole.

But companies can reduce the published profit figure by various accounting techniques. These are explained in Chapter 13. The meaning and uses of other parts of the accounts are explained in Chapters 9, 10 and 11.

# 5.

# The profits of a subsidiary

You are employed by the subsidiary of a public company. It is a limited liability company; therefore it has to produce separate accounts. These will be kept at Companies House. The profit will be shown in the Profit and Loss Account. Chapter 4 explains how to work out the surplus from the Profit and Loss Account.

If you want a more detailed explanation of the terms in the Profit and Loss Account, read Chapter 10.

## Limitations of accounts:

The accounts of subsidiary companies have several limitations:

■ **The company may not file the annual accounts.** Although the law requires a limited company to file its annual return (which includes the accounts) within twelve months of the end of the financial year, many do not do so. Public companies usually do. They run the risk of losing the quotation for their shares if they are very slow in producing their final figures. As a result of this and because lateness will discredit the management, public companies are rarely late in producing their annual accounts. It is very different with the accounts of their subsidiaries.

Of the 550,000 active companies registered at Companies House tens of thousands are late in making their return. These companies are not just small private companies; some are the subsidiaries of large public companies. And the Department of Trade, which is responsible for enforcing company law, is slow at following them up.

■ **The accounts may not show the real profits.** As far as the shareholder is concerned, the only important figure is the profit figure for the whole of a group. The shareholder is not much concerned with the profitability of one particular subsidiary. He is only interested in the total profit. Directors, however, may wish to hide the profitability of any particular division, to keep information from its competitors, customers, workers or the government.

> ■ T. Wall & Sons, the meat pie and sausage company, is a subsidiary of Unilever. Its accounts show sales in 1972 of £71.59 million, but a loss of £585,000, compared to a profit of £268,000 in the year before. In 1957, when the company was much smaller, but had only just been taken over by Unilever, profits were £2,042,000. Unilever has hidden the real profitability of Walls.

> ■ Associated Container Transportation (Services) Ltd is not a small company. It has 463 employees. It describes its business as 'providing services connected with the operation of container transport'. In 1972, its first year of operation, turnover was £7.9 million. But its profit was only £8,816. The company is owned by five shipping companies all of whom are its customers.

# Hiding the profit:

If the directors wish to hide the profit of a subsidiary, these are the ways in which it can be done:

## Pricing:

In intercompany sales one subsidiary can charge crippling prices to another subsidiary in the group: the profits of the subsidiary buying the product will then disappear. The alternative is for the supplying company to charge low prices, to depress its own profits. For the directors, who know the reasons for the low profits, and can quantify exactly the cost of the high prices, it doesn't matter. But the worker looking at the accounts may be inclined to believe management claims that the company is unprofitable.

> 'The Standard Oil Company of Ohio (Sohio) was today accused of boosting the profits of British Petroleum, its Affiliate, by buying high-priced crude oil from the British

*company.*
*Senator Howard Metzenbaum, a Democrat from Ohio, said in a statement that according to information he received privately Sohio paid BP more for its Iranian light crude oil than it paid for similar oil from other suppliers.*
*'British Petroleum owns 25 per cent of the American company and will control it by 1977.*
*'The senator said Sohio refused to disclose its oil purchasing policies.*
*'If Sohio did disclose the facts, we would understand the relationship between the company's relatively modest profit increases by oil industry standards, and the astounding profits of British Petroleum,' Senator Metzenbaum said.*
*'He added: "We could only conclude that Sohio has been victimising the gas-buying (petrol-buying) public to boost the profits of British Petroleum – a notorious example of the harmful consequences of self-dealing between American oil companies and their foreign affiliates." – Reuter report, 6 June 1974.*

## Contribution to group expenses:

The parent company will make a charge for the subsidiary's contribution to the expenses of the whole group – the expense of having a head office and so on.

■ In the T. Wall & Son Accounts, it says that Unilever makes a management charge to the company.

The clues (but only clues) to the operation of a discriminatory pricing policy are:

■ Statements that the parent company makes a management charge, or the lack of any directors' fees. If there are no directors' fees, it means that the directors are paid by the parent company. This suggests that the subsidiary is not regarded as a separate company for accounting purposes.

■ The balance sheet position. What is the main source of finance for the company: is it its own retained profits or is it a loan from the parent company? The subsidiary will have been allowed to retain its profits if it was considered a separate accounting entity.

In the Walls and ACT Balance Sheets there is evidence that the main source of capital was from the parent company.

■ In the T. Wall Balance Sheet, there is a loan from the holding company of £20,889,000. In the ACT Balance Sheet there is a loan of £1,434,000 from the shareholders compared to total net assets of under £200,000.

The practice of charging intergroup expenses is used particularly between countries, as a way of redistributing profits from a high-tax country to a low-tax country; as a way of overcoming restrictions on the movement of capital and as a way of avoiding profit restrictions imposed by any government. This is why it is important to concentrate on the parent company profit.

> ■ Tampax Ltd is 81 per cent owned by the American company, Tampax Inc. M.J.H. Nightingale, a firm of UK bankers, wrote in a confidential document: 'Among the uncertainties which an investor in Tampax Ltd must accept is a possible change in overall corporate policy especially as regards intercompany pricing which could affect the United Kingdom subsidiary's profitability.'
> ■ In 1973 Peter Dixon, a Grimsby-based manufacturer of newsprint, announced it was to close its factory and make 900 people redundant. The company claimed that the mill was losing £700,000 a year. One of the mill's suppliers of pulp was the Peter Dixon pulp mill in Finland. Its profits exceeded £350,000 a year.

It is difficult to be sure if companies are redistributing profits in this way but always check if there are companies in the same group as the one you work for that could be intergroup suppliers. A list of subsidiaries can be obtained from the annual accounts of the whole group.

Because of the opportunity for depressing profits in a particular subsidiary, the accounts of a subsidiary should not be relied upon as a guide to the real profit. Concentrate on the profits of the whole group if the profits of the particular subsidiary seem very low. Chapter 4 tells you how to understand the Profit and Loss Account of a public company.

If you work for a subsidiary company and the management want to close it down because it is unprofitable, or sack workers to make it more profitable, look at the history of the subsidiary. The company's ability to generate profits may be affected in three ways:

■ The level of dividends paid out in the past. If all the profits have been paid in dividends to the parent company the subsidiary will be much weaker than if it had been allowed to keep its profits.

■ Has the subsidiary made any loans to the parent or other companies in the group? If these were made at very low rates of interest then that subsidiary's profits would have been reduced.

■ Has the subsidiary paid rent or management charges to other parts of the group? If it has, profits will have been reduced.

# Why subsidiaries?

Why do companies have separate limited subsidiaries? There are two main reasons:

■ **The protection of limited liability extended to the subsidiaries.** The subsidiary companies can go bankrupt without the parent company losing anything but the original money that is put up – the equity or share capital – and any inter-company indebtedness, such as loans.

Anxiety to protect its own self-interest will normally restrain a firm from using the protection of limited liability to the full: people doing business with a subsidiary of a major company will assume that they are doing business with the larger and stronger parent company. Any attempt by the parent to hide behind the protection of limited liability will damage the company's name substantially and make other companies less likely to do business with it.

■ **It is frequently easier to run a company if each activity is established in separate companies.**

■ Sainsbury's and four other companies have formed a joint company with £3000 of equity capital to develop property they own along the River Thames. Nearly all property companies establish a new company for each major development.

Giving each activity of a company a separate identity – as a limited company – makes it easier to identify the costs of running it.

It also makes it easier to sell the company: What is being sold is the share capital of a company that runs a business and owns some assets. This is easier to value and simpler to carry out than valuing a collection of debts, property, stocks, trade marks, that are not held together in one specific company.

When companies turn divisions of a company into specific limited companies it is sometimes a sign of an attempt by management to isolate the relative profitability of different activities.

## Summary:

Dividing the business into limited subsidiaries keeps open two important options for a company: the protection of limited liability in the case of bankruptcy and easy sale of a company if such a step seems appropriate at any time. Often it's just easier to do it that way.

# 6.

# The profits of a private company

A private company has to produce annual Reports and Accounts. These are available at Companies House. But first check that the company is not a public unquoted company, which has a card in the Extel unquoted service, as this may be more readily available than Companies House.

Chapter 4 shows how to establish the size of the surplus from the Profit and Loss Account.

But private companies have special ways of reducing the profit figure and therefore particular characteristics.

## Concealing profits from the taxman:

There are special reasons for making profits appear low.

The **public company** has shareholders to satisfy who are in no way connected with the management of the company. Many of these shareholders simply want to see their company producing profits, even if some of it has to be paid to the taxman.

**Private companies** are generally owned by the directors. Even when they are not, the shareholders will be in very close contact with the management and will know what the real profits are, whatever the Report and Accounts may show. The most important consideration for private companies is to minimize payment to the taxman.

The private company is helped in this tax avoidance by the firm's accountants, who audit the accounts. Auditors are appointed by the shareholders. In public companies, because they are open to greater public scrutiny and it is not good for any auditor's reputation if it is shown that the rules are not being kept, there is still some pressure on the auditors to maintain some independence from the directors.

None of this applies to a private company. The auditors are frequently advising the firm on day-to-day management. They are paid by the directors in their role as shareholders. They will co-operate in any tax minimizing activity. If they don't they may lose their job.

# Minimum information:

As a result of this desire to minimize the amount of money paid to the taxman, the information supplied in the accounts of private companies is often meagre and misleading.

**Especially:**
Companies are not so likely to revalue any property assets, so the balance sheet is not a safe guide to the wealth of the company.

The 1972 Balance Sheet of the private Woolcroft Estates showed assets of £3,213. In March 1973 it was decided to put the company into voluntary liquidation. The assets were declared to be worth £570,661.

Corby's Ltd, a private company manufacturing trouser presses, showed property of £24,000 in its 1972 Balance Sheet. A year later this was valued at £100,000.

Companies are more likely to use any or all of the techniques of understating profits listed in Chapter 13, especially the technique of hiding profits in the stock figure (pages 154–57.)

# Transfer pricing:

Private companies are just as likely to redistribute profits between companies within a group as public companies (page 63); but there is an added complication with private companies; profits may be redirected between companies that are apparently unconnected, but in fact have the same shareholders. It is not always possible to tell if there is another company connected with the one you are researching.

In any bargaining situation the worker needs to know the profitability and wealth of the owners of the company he works for. In a public company this is comparatively easy: the accounts of the parent company are the source of information. In the case of a private company it is harder as there may not be one company that holds all the business interests of the owners. They will probably have their business interests in a series of separate companies.

To establish the wealth – and therefore the real profit – look at the list of the directors' other directorships which should be in the file at Companies House. Look up each of these companies and see if the lists of shareholders are similar to those in the particular company in which you are interested.

This is not a foolproof method because people can own companies and not be directors of them. There are some other ways in which you can discover connexions between companies that do not have any directors or shareholders in common. The most useful guide is often the source of loans to the company.

> ▣ Leeford (London) Ltd is a small engineering company near Fakenham. It is owned by Heinrich Fritz Liebrecht and his wife. In 1974 workers at the company suspected that there was some connexion with Howard Rotavator, which was the company's main customer.
>
> The Balance Sheet of Leeford showed that the company was largely financed by £42,000 of loans. Examination of the company's mortgage deeds at Companies House showed that Howard Rotavator had made Leeford an £11,500 loan, convertible into shares; that Howard Rotavator had a mortgage on the company's property; that it had been lending the company money since 1964 and that it had even allowed Leefords to fall £2,434 into arrears with loan repayments.
>
> Whoever owned the shares of Leefords, the company was clearly controlled by Howard Rotavator. As Howard Rotavator was the company's main customer, Leeford's apparently low profits of £9,306 were of little relevance.

**When companies are in the same or connected business, profits can be easily distributed between companies by the pricing structure.**

■ Richard Tompkins owns 97.5 per cent of the Green Shield Company, which is a private company. He is the director of several other private companies and also of the public company New Day Holdings. New Day has a subsidiary called Argos which operates a chain of discount stores. Argos is financed by interest-free loans from Green Shield and receives important management help such as warehouse facilities and catalogues, free of charge. The result of this arrangement is that profits are re-distributed from Green Shield to Argos. Tompkins does this because New Day is a public company in which he holds several million shares. If its profits increase and the share price rises Tompkins will get richer. If he ever sells any of these shares the maximum tax he will have to pay is 30 per cent capital gains tax on the profit he makes. In Green Shield, he has to pay tax as high as 90 per cent on his £250,000 annual salary and on the dividends he pays himself.

■ Alfred Teddy Smith, banker and property developer, has several private property companies. Not all of them appear very profitable. But in total the private companies he owns are financed by £1.6 million of loans from Bryanston Finance, a public company which he controls. So the lack of profitability of the private companies is partly due to increasing the public company's profits. He increases these further by making loans – very cheaply – from other private companies he controls.

If interest charges in a private company's accounts appear very high, or the bank overdraft is high, check whether the money is being provided by a company with which the directors are connected. If the overdrafts are secured against property, there should be a record of the lender in the back of the company's file, in the mortgage documents.

# Directors' fees and expenses:

One of the ways to reduce the pretax profit of a company is by paying the directors more wages and by allowing them various perks – such as cars or houses. It will be easy to see from the Notes to the Accounts how the directors' fees have changed, and these should anyway be added in to the pretax profit figure to establish the size of the surplus.

There is no obligation to show the value of non-monetary benefits, though some companies do so, and it should be checked. The tax charge may provide a clue to the extent of some of these benefits: see page 102 below.

Look in the Balance Sheet and see if there are any motor vehicles listed as assets. From your own knowledge, does the company have any motor vehicles? It is very common in private (and public) companies for the company to own the directors' cars.

These are the problems that will be encountered in trying to find the size of real profits from the accounts of private companies. In addition, the accounts may be very much out of date and, especially if the company is small, profits may have increased substantially since the last accounts.

Chapter 13 lists some of the commonest ways in which profits can be understated.

# 7.

# The profits of a nationalized enterprise

Find a copy of the annual accounts of the enterprise. Chapter 3 tells you how to do this.

Find the **Consolidated Profit and Loss Account.** Read Chapter 4 of this book which tells you how to establish the size of the real profit from the Profit and Loss Account.

There is much more information in the accounts of nationalized enterprises than in the accounts of private industry. This can make it difficult to find the figures needed to establish the size of the real profit, so read the accounts very carefully. The information can often be used to find out increases in productivity, the extent of industrial accidents, and other management information, not normally available in annual accounts.

■ The British Rail accounts show that during 1972 the labour force fell by a larger percentage than the amount of traffic: i.e. workers were doing more work than in the previous year. Productivity had increased.
■ The NCB accounts show that in 1973, 80 miners were killed, compared to 58 in 1972. There were 69,000 accidents, compared to 64,540 in 1972.

There are four reasons why nationalized enterprises' profits appear lower than those of private industry: they are described below.

# Capital structure:

The nationalized industries have no shareholders. Although they are allowed to run themselves as capitalist corporations they do not have the same capital structure. The balance sheets show that they are financed almost entirely by government loans, which means that interest charges are very high.

In a conventional private enterprise company, there are two groups of capitalists – shareholders, who receive dividends, and the loan stock holders, who get interest payments. The dividends are paid from after-tax profits. Interest on loans is paid from pretax profits. Because the nationalized industries are all financed by loan capital, the interest charged is much higher than it would be in a private sector company.

■ Pages 75 and 77 show the Balance Sheets of the Post Office and Laporte Industries – the company which sends misleading accounts to its workers (see page 14). Although the Post Office is much bigger than Laporte, Laporte's capital structure is fairly typical of much of British industry. You can see from the Laporte Balance Sheet that of £70,675,000 of long-term finance, £25.6 million is in the form of loans and £37.7 million comes from the ordinary shareholders, the preference shareholders and from retained profits, which belong to the ordinary shareholders.

The Post Office accounts show that £3,043 million – or 75 per cent – of its £4,074 million long-term finance is in the form of loans. If, like Laporte, only 36 per cent of its long-term money came from loans, then the long-term interest bill in 1974 would have been £113 million, instead of £230 million and profits would have been £123 million instead of £5.2 million.

The point is that the state would receive any money made by the Post Office – either in taxes or in dividends, as its only shareholder. So the level of pre-tax profits is unimportant. What is important is that these profits should not be depressed by subsidizing private industry through low prices. If it is a good thing to subsidize private industry, the full cost must be spelt out very clearly, so that the lack of profits does not mean that the nationalized industries are starved of money needed for capital investment. In fact, as demonstrated below, among the major reasons for the lack of profitability of the nationalized industries are low prices, their accounting policies and decent pensions.

Laporte Industries : Balance sheet

## Consolidated Balance Sheet

at 30th December 1973

| | Notes | 1973 £'000 | 1973 £'000 | 1972 £'000 | 1972 £'000 |
|---|---|---|---|---|---|
| **Assets employed:** | | | | | |
| Fixed assets | 10 | | 33,547 | | 34,948 |
| Goodwill | | | 4,694 | | 4,694 |
| Investments | 11 | | 7,541 | | 5,807 |
| Current assets | | | | | |
| Stocks | 12 | 10,702 | | 11,254 | |
| Debtors | | 15,336 | | 13,654 | |
| Short-term loans and bank balances | | 9,289 | | 3,946 | |
| | | 35,327 | | 28,854 | |
| Current liabilities | 13 | 10,434 | | 7,295 | |
| Net current assets | | | 24,893 | | 21,559 |
| | | | 70,675 | | 67,108 |
| **Financed by:** | | | | | |
| Ordinary shareholders' funds | | | | | |
| Ordinary share capital | 14 | | 16,075 | | 16,075 |
| Share premium | 15 | | 4,569 | | 4,569 |
| Reserves | | | 16,308 | | 13,445 |
| | | | 36,952 | | 34,089 |
| Preference stock | 16 | | 771 | | 771 |
| Deferred taxation | 17 | | 4,667 | | 3,866 |
| Investment and development grants | 18 | | 2,645 | | 3,014 |
| Loans | 19 | | 10,605 | | 10,129 |
| Debenture stock | | | 15,035 | | 15,239 |
| | | | 70,675 | | 67,108 |

So, it is particularly important in the case of a nationalized industry to add the interest to the pre-tax profit or loss to establish the size of the surplus produced by the workers.

This interest is paid to the government. In some cases it may seem very high because it incorporates repayment of the capital debt as well, which a company in the private sector normally does not do.

■ The NCB is to start repaying £413 million over 20 years in 1973/4.

**Remember:**

Most of these loans are the legacy of the money that was paid by the government when industries were nationalized. This means that the nationalized industries are still labouring under the pressure to make a 'decent' return for the shareholders of the old private companies.

# Aid to private industry:

The nationalized industries make losses, so that private industry can profit.

Although in theory the nationalized industries are run independently of the government, the one area in which the government frequently intervenes is pricing. Prices are often held down, bringing unprofitability, and wages are held down to keep prices down. The profits of the industries' privately owned customers increase because of these low prices.

■ Between 1970 and 1973 government control of prices cost the Electricity Council at least £165 million. During the same period gross trading profits of privately owned industry increased from £5,279 million to £6,584 million. 59 per cent of electricity is consumed by business. Fifty-three per cent of the NCB's coal goes to electricity power stations. A further nine per cent goes directly to industry. In 1973 the NCB lost £83.3 million.
■ In 1974 the Post Office made a loss of £128 million. But this was largely a result of holding down prices. The government paid the Post Office £133 million compensation, so that profits were £5 million.

If the interest paid on loans is added back, as it should be, most nationalized industries make big profits. Do not forget that the nationalized industries serve profit-making private industry much more than they serve the domestic consumer.

## Post Office balance sheet
at 31 March 1974

| | £'000 | £'000 | 1973 £'000 |
|---|---|---|---|
| **NET ASSETS** | | | |
| Fixed assets (Note 13) | | 4 163 175 | 3 658 608 |
| Telecommunications investment in Intelsat (Note 14) | | 10 183 | 8 466 |
| Giro investments other than short-term (Note 15) | | 65 728 | 52 222 |
| DPS computer projects (Note 16) | | 2 034 | 2 375 |
| **Current assets** | | | |
| Stocks (Note 18) | 13 754 | | 13 358 |
| Debtors | 399 882 | | 255 088 |
| Compensation (Note 3) | 123 567 | | — |
| Cash and short-term funds | 146 322 | | 137 671 |
| | 683 525 | | 406 117 |
| **Current liabilities** | | | |
| Creditors (Note 20) | 422 894 | | 279 757 |
| Giro customer balances (Note 21) | 85 041 | | 58 344 |
| Agency service balances | 60 390 | | 82 496 |
| Uncashed postal and money orders (Note 22) | 24 041 | | 23 901 |
| Short-term loans from Minister* | 200 000 | | — |
| Bank advances | 58 242 | | 26 116 |
| | 850 608 | | 470 614 |
| Net current liabilities | | (167 083) | (64 497) |
| | | 4 074 037 | 3 657 174 |
| **FINANCED BY** | | | |
| Loans from Minister* (Note 24) | | 2 818 974 | 2 752 418 |
| Foreign loans (Note 25) | | 224 369 | 10 280 |
| General reserve (Note 27) | | 1 030 894 | 894 476 |
| | | 4 074 037 | 3 657 174 |

A. W. C. RYLAND  Chairman

A. E. SINGER  Member

*Subsequent to 31 March 1974 redesignated as loans from Secretary of State.

# Depreciation policy:

Several of the nationalized industries use a depreciation policy that makes allowance for inflation: instead of calculating depreciation on the basis of the cost of its assets, it is calculated on the basis of the replacement cost. This ensures that the industry accumulates sufficient funds to replace its assets. Very few companies in the private sector do this, so that their profits will tend to appear higher than those of nationalized industries.

> ■ In 1974, the Post Office charged £84.2 million supplementary depreciation 'to bring the annual depreciation charge into line with depreciation on replacement cost'.

# Pension funds:

Several of the nationalized industries have just started to put their pension funds on a 'sound financial footing'. This costs money. This money is taken from the trading profits. The result is that real profits are low because the industries are having to pay for the mismanagement of the pension fund in the past.

> ■ In 1974 the Post Office paid a £98 million deficiency payment to the pension fund. This was not the Post Office's annual contribution as an employer to the fund (which amounted to an extra £51 million) but an exceptional charge to make up for the money that had been robbed from the fund in the past. In the previous year the deficiency charge had been only £44.3 million.
>
> These expenses, although they are to continue for years, are 'exceptional'. They are in no way related to the labour of the Post Office workers. They are the result of managerial incompetence. Look for such exceptional items and add them to the pre-tax profits, to arrive at the figure for the surplus.

No company in the private sector has to make pensions payments of this size. Many companies in the private sector do not even provide their employees with a pension and even those companies that do rarely ensure that the pension is inflation-proof, which the Post Office pension almost is. One of the reasons why the nationalized industries' profits are low is because they make some attempt to provide a half decent pension for their workers.

When the Post Office produced its 1974 Accounts, the press reported that it had lost £128 million. To put the accounts on a comparable basis with those of private industry, you can do the following calculations:

|                                            | £ million |
|--------------------------------------------|-----------|
| PO reported loss                           | 128       |
| Less: Government compensation for price restraint | 133 |
| Profit:                                    | 5         |
| Add:                                       |           |
| Adjustment for capital structure           | 127       |
| Excess depreciation                        | 84        |
| Pension deficiency                         | 98        |
| Profit:                                    | 314       |

And this is just to arrive at the profit figure. The surplus is much higher.

Now – read Chapter 4, which tells you how to establish the size of the surplus.

# Part Two:

What company
accounts reveal –

and conceal

# 8.

# What companies are obliged to disclose

There are six important sets of documents which a limited liability company has to file with the Registrar of Companies, at Companies House (part of the Department of Industry):

- A copy of the Articles of Association
- A copy of the Memorandum of Association
- A list of the directors, with a list of their other directorships
- A list of the shareholders
- The annual Report and Accounts
- A list of mortgages

## Articles of Association:

These are the **internal regulations** by which the company is to be run. They are very similar for all companies, as the law has a standard form which most companies find convenient to use.

## Memorandum of Association:

These are the **conditions on which the company is formed.** They list the registered office of the company, the name and the business of the company. It is against the law for the company to carry on any business other than that listed in the Memorandum. The activities can only be altered with the permission of the holders of 75 per cent of the company's shares.

The existence of the Memorandum and Articles may make it sound as though company directors are very restricted in the way they run companies. This is not the case.

Memoranda are always drawn up in terms as general as possible, so that every conceivable type of business is covered. Rules governing the management of companies can be changed with the agreement of the shareholders. However impressive the paraphernalia of registered companies sounds, the reality is that in most respects companies are self-governing.

# Shareholders and directors:

The list of shareholders and directors' other directorships is available at Companies House: It is not produced in the Annual Report.

# Annual Reports and Accounts:

Companies are required by the Companies Acts of 1948 and 1967 to publish an annual Report and Accounts. Companies quoted on the Stock Exchange, which are all public companies, are required to send a report to their shareholders every 12 months. A few large private companies (Heron Corporation, for example) produce accounts with the same sort of information and presentation as public companies, though they are not obliged to do so.

**The general idea of the accounts** is 'to give a true and fair view of the state of affairs and profit of the company, as it concerns the shareholders'. This is often different from the view of the company shown to the taxman, or presented to the workers. Specifically, the main requirements are:
- A notice summoning the Annual General Meeting
- The Directors' Report
- The Consolidated Profit and Loss Account
- Consolidated Balance Sheet
- Profit and Loss and Balance Sheet of the parent company
- List of subsidiaries
- The Auditor's Report

These provisions may sound exhaustive, but in practice companies vary widely in the amount of information they provide and the accuracy with which they give a fair and honest view of the company. The organization of Reports and Accounts also varies substantially, but normally the information will appear in the order given above. Additionally, although there is no statutory obligation, most companies produce a Chairman's statement which reports on the year's progress and often provides the Chairman with an excuse for airing some of his prejudices.

The information that companies are required to show in the Report and Accounts is detailed. It is explained fully in the following three chapters:

Chapter 9: The Directors' Report
Chapter 10: The Profit and Loss Account
Chapter 11: The Balance Sheet

The way in which the information is organized varies from company to company. A lot of the information will be in the Notes to the Accounts, which follow the Balance Sheets and the Profit and Loss Accounts.

Appendix 2 gives a complete list of Companies Act and Stock Exchange requirements for the disclosure of information.

# 9.

# The Directors' Report

## The Annual General Meeting:

The main purposes of the AGM are:
- To receive the Directors' Report
- To declare the final dividend
- To elect the directors
- To appoint the auditors

The AGM also gives an opportunity to ask questions of the directors. Because companies are normally profitable and the shareholders therefore happy, most AGMs are a formality with the attendance most nearly related to the amount of food and drink provided. However, recently some groups have been able to use the AGM to draw attention to a company's involvement in South Africa, redundancy plans, etc. Only shareholders can attend AGMs, but one share is sufficient qualification.

The following list covers the main information that should be included in the Directors' Report:
- Description of the company's main activities
- Any changes in the assets of the company during the year
- Any shares issues during the year
- Interest of any directors in any contract that the company has entered into during the year
- A breakdown of turnover (sales) and profit by different activities
- Political and charitable contributions
- Amounts paid out in dividends and amount of profit retained
- Exports

- Names of directors and their pay
- Details of any share option schemes open to directors
- Directors' interest in the company's shares
- Average number of UK employees and their total pay

### The main activities of the company:

The law requires the company to mention any significant change in the activities of the company during the year. These requirements are clearly general and open to the most liberal interpretation. A company manufacturing screws, nuts, bolts, door hinges, etc., can itemize these activities, or just say 'a wide range of engineering products' or even 'engineering'. Failure to describe the business is widespread: a survey of published accounts for 1973–74, made by the General Educational Trust of the English Institute, showed that of the 300 biggest public companies in Britain, although 222 gave an analysis of sales and profits, 78 provided no analysis or comment.

> In its 1973 accounts Wimpey described its business as 'construction'. This gives no indication that the company owns substantial property developments and that it builds oil drilling platforms as well as houses.
> In its 1973 accounts Howard Tenens said that its principal activities were 'The provision of an integrated service covering warehousing, casemaking, processing, packaging, transportation in the UK and abroad and the manufacture of pressings, sub-assemblies and bodies for the motor industry'. It did not say that £150,000 of its £806,000 pretax profit came in the form of rental income from property it owned.

It is important to know exactly what business your employer is in. If a construction company is not just in house building its profits are unlikely to fall so dramatically when there is a house-building slump. If a company has substantial rental income it is less reliant on its trading operations for survival. This means it can survive difficult trading conditions longer and resist pressure from workers longer.

### Secondary banks:

A particularly misleading description of a company's business can be 'banking'.

There is an increasing number of companies calling themselves bankers or 'investment bankers'. These should not be confused with the four main 'clearing banks' which have branches in towns up and down the country. Many companies that are involved in the lending of money, however specialized or however expensive that may be, are calling themselves 'banks' in a lust for respectability.

These **secondary banks**, as they are called, encountered serious financial problems in the last half of 1973 and in 1974. What happened was quite simple. These companies relied heavily on the money market for their deposits.

The money market is a curious organization that exists in series of telephone calls. Companies and other organizations with large amounts of money can lend for short periods of time, through the services of a money broker, on the money market. The secondary banks, who were the main borrowers, were lending this money very heavily to property developers.

In the last half of 1973, interest rates increased dramatically and property prices started falling. The companies that were lending money to the secondary banks, through the money market, realized that the security of the banks' loans was declining and withdrew their money. The banks could not easily get their money back as much of the property it was financing was not easy to sell.

To save the whole banking system from collapsing, the major clearing banks and the Bank of England came to the rescue. The secondary banks still survive.

The two most important differences between them and the four major clearing banks are:

■ The secondary banks take a more active interest in their customers' business – often taking a share of the profits, bringing them deals, or arranging takeovers.

■ The secondary banks generally charge more for overdrafts.

■ London & County Securities, one of the banking outfits that crashed in 1973, had shareholdings of over 10 per cent in ten companies – including Drake & Cubitts, the builders, and Westons, the chemists. In 1972 London and County lent International Property Development £2 million to buy the Fisher Bendix factory in Liverpool and charged £225,000 for the service.

The involvements of banks – including the clearing banks – directly in business is likely to increase with the expansion of financially inexperienced companies into Europe, greater competitive pressure and the need for long term finance, unavailable elsewhere.

The growing importance of financial companies, involvement in productive industry is an important development for workers. The investment banker has little interest in the business he is running. He will quickly close businesses if he thinks that he can make money elsewhere. Not that this is not carried on by businessmen every day, but it is the hallmark of the 'investment banker'. He will take a much shorter term view than many businessmen who do feel some commitment to the business they run.

**If a company describes banking as its principal activity, check further. If a company mentions its connexion with one of these banks, it is a clue to the style of the management.**

### Changes in assets:

There will be a table – probably in the Notes to the Accounts – showing changes in the company's assets during the year. Companies are not obliged to show where the money has been spent, whether abroad, in the UK, or in which subsidiary. It is sometimes possible to find out in which particular parts of the business the company is investing by looking at the balance sheets of the individual subsidiaries in Companies House.

■ Between 1963 and 1972, Tate & Lyle increased its fixed assets from £66 million to £114 million. But an examination of the accounts of Tate & Lyle Refineries Ltd – the company which includes the UK sugar refining operation – shows that less than £1 million of this was invested in their UK refining capacity.

Throughout this period Tate & Lyle were asking the government for help to protect their UK sugar business against foreign competition. As a report by a firm of stockbrokers said: 'Sugar refining is to be used as "a cash cow" and divisions in which investment will be particularly strong are storage, multiple distribution and warehousing, engineering (particularly in Canada) and specialized shipping.' All of these are activities with a small labour force or are outside Britain.

Revaluation of assets should be commented upon in the Report but the amount of information provided varies enormously from company to company. There is no statutory obligation for companies to revalue their assets at regular intervals.

The asset most likely to be affected by revaluation is freehold property, which has consistently risen in value over the years. Companies are not required to state the date on which they acquired property and such assets may just appear 'at cost', in the Notes to the Balance Sheet. The fact that there is no reference to any increase in the value of the assets does not mean that the property is not worth substantially more than the accounts say.

Do not necessarily believe the directors if they say that in their opinion the market value of the property is not materially different from that appearing in the accounts. The valuation of property is very subjective, especially if the valuation takes into account the development value of the property. Often the directors will make such statements to discourage a possible bidder with his eye on the company's property.

Be wary of the basis on which some valuations are made. Sometimes the directors may say that the property has been valued 'on a going concern basis'. Suppose a company owns an empty warehouse by the River Thames. Valued as such – its going concern basis – it may not be very valuable. But if it is next to a major development, or could be turned into offices, then it will be worth much more.

An accurate valuation of the company's assets is important because it is often the largest part of the company's wealth, affecting its ability to survive slack trading conditions when it might otherwise sack workers. A company with freehold property will find it easier to borrow money, using the property as security. The bank manager, needless to say, won't pay much attention to the book value of the property but to its market value.

For this reason be wary of asset-stripping operations where the property is sold, even though the conventional manufacturing is allowed to continue undisturbed. If things get difficult, the company has nothing to fall back upon, having sold its most valuable asset. The company will have little strength to survive a period of losses. To maintain profits and keep the business going, workers will be sacked (see pages 174–175).

There is one occasion on which land and property may appear as a current asset at well below its real value.

This is where a company is holding land for redevelopment, such as building. In the private house building boom of 1971/2 several companies were lucky enough to have a 'land bank' at the beginning and made money from the increase in the value of the land alone. This type of increase in the value of assets would not be mentioned and you should look in the Balance Sheet, to see if the company is holding any land or buildings as current assets.

### Share issues:

The company will say what shares have been issued during the year and why. But if it says that another company has been acquired for (say) 1,000 shares, it should be remembered that the value of the deal is worked out from the market price of those shares, that is, their price on the Stock Market on the day the deal was concluded. This will probably not be given in the Report and Accounts.

### Directors' interests:

The report should list the interests of any directors in any significant contracts made by the company during the year.

An example of this could be as follows: a company has agreed to buy a building that is owned by a director in his personal capacity. The word 'significant' leaves an enormous amount of discretion to the directors and accountants, and it is unusual to find a record of such contracts. Agreements between the company and a relation of the directors, (say) brother-in-law of the Chairman, need not be disclosed.

■ Laurie Marsh Group 1972 Report and Accounts. The Directors' Report gives details of five acquisitions. One of these was Town Markets Ltd, vendors L.P. Marsh and D.L. Young. Marsh received 572,310 shares in his company Laurie Marsh, valued at approximately £700,000. The details are baldly stated, no attention being drawn to the fact that L.P. Marsh is the Chairman of the Laurie Marsh Group. This is one small way of diverting attention from specific pieces of information.

If there is a declaration of a director's interest see if there is any reference to how the company decided what price to pay for the acquisition. If the price was not established by an independent third party, the directors may not have been absolutely impartial in the price they paid.

### Breakdown of turnover and profit:

The report should itemize turnover and profit for activities that are substantially different. There is considerable scope for directors to interpret 'substantially' as they wish. But if a company is (say) a property developer and a manufacturer of dresses, the directors will rarely dare to treat these as the same business.

Some companies are willing to give a breakdown of turnover, but not profits. They frequently claim it is to prevent competitors discovering their profitability. It also helps keep workers uninformed.

Banks and discount houses are exempt from this provision. This stems from their right not to disclose their real profits. Up to 1969 the big four banks used to show their profit 'after tax and transfer to inner reserves'. The inner reserves were not disclosed. It was once felt that if banks showed their real profit, which might rise and fall from year to year, depositors would withdraw all their money from the bank in a bad year, out of fear the bank was going bust. With the banks financing so much of industry, the results could be disastrous.

By 1969 it was obvious that banks were rich enough not to worry about this, and apparently on their own initiative, though probably under pressure from the Labour government, they decided to disclose their true profit.

Many merchant banks, however, still make use of this handy law, so it is impossible to establish their true profit.

### Political and charitable donations:

Political parties have to be listed by name; charities do not. This means that certain quasi-political organizations may escape mention. Though most companies recognize that the Economic League is a political organization.

### Dividend recommendation:

In theory the shareholders own the company and so they have to approve the payment of a dividend at the AGM. In fact the directors decide what dividend is going to be paid. The shareholders rarely complain. At the moment government policy restricts dividend increases, although payments may exceed restriction for a variety of reasons.

### Exports:

Only sales need be given. Some companies give a breakdown by country. If a company can persuade the Department of Industry that it isn't in the national interest to disclose the value of exports, they are exempted from this provision. Lesney, manufacturers of Matchbox toys, is one company that has this dispensation: its exports to America are substantial.

### Directors' names and pay:

Any changes in directorship should be listed. Shareholdings and a summary of salaries must be shown but will often appear in the Notes to the Accounts. Only the Chairman's pay can be specifically identified. There is no requirement to list the directors' other directorships in the Report and Accounts, but the company's file at Companies House should have this information.

Companies are obliged to keep a statement of directors' transactions in the company's shares at the registered office of the company. The address can be obtained from the Extel card or *Stock Exchange Year-Book*. Anyone has the right to inspect this during regular business hours, between the date of the publication of a company's accounts and the AGM.

### Share incentive schemes:

The tax system has put some sort of ceiling on the salaries company directors can be paid. Companies have therefore devised share option or share incentive schemes that give their directors and senior executives the opportunity to buy shares in their company either for a purely nominal amount, or with money borrowed from the company.

The profits on these share incentive schemes are subject to capital gains tax, which at 30 per cent is much lower than income tax, which can be higher than 70 per cent.

> One company with a share incentive scheme is Hill Samuel. Under the terms of their scheme directors made large sums of money in 1972 and 1973.
>
> The scheme worked as follows: Directors paid a nominal amount of money to buy an option on shares in the company. That gave them the right to buy the shares at any time in the future, after three years had elapsed. The price they paid was the price of the shares on the day they took out the option.
>
> Under this scheme, in November and December 1972, director Robert Clark bought 35,000 shares at 63p. Within days these were sold at 180p each. Director H.R. Moore bought 70,000 at the same price and sold them at around 180p. Sir Kenneth Keith bought 400,000 at 63p.

Look at the incentive scheme and, if sufficient information is given, work out how much a director stands to make and what his outlay is; directors have to show the number of shares over which they have options.

If the full details of the scheme are not given in the Report and Accounts it may be necessary to contact the company or their Registrars to obtain a copy of the document that was sent out with details of the scheme to be approved by shareholders.

Remember that such schemes are often open to senior executives who are not members of the Board. There is no obligation for companies to name the executives who benefit.

Under legislation introduced by the Labour government in 1974 the introduction of *new* share incentive schemes has been frozen.

### Directors' shareholdings:

Directors are obliged to disclose the number of shares that they own in the company. They must also disclose any shares that are held in trust, of which they are trustees. These holdings are called 'non-beneficial'.

Knowledge of the directors' shareholdings and changes in them is helpful:

■ It is possible to work out the wealth of the directors from their shareholding, and how much personal interest they have in the company. This might explain the low pay they receive. From the shareholdings it is possible to work out how much they receive in dividends, in addition to their salaries.

■ If the directors have been selling shares, it may be because things have been going wrong.

> ■ Between March 1972 and March 1973, Freddie Strasser, Chairman of Nova Jersey, reduced his holding in the company from 942,000 to 896,000 shares. Profits fell from £961,000 to £436,000.

For some obscure and totally confusing reason, shares held jointly, either beneficially or non-beneficially, appear as separate holdings for each of the directors. Although there is a requirement to declare that some holdings are jointly held, the exact number of shares does not need to be mentioned.

**Directors do not have to disclose the interests of their families.**

> ■ Jeffery Pike of Tremletts. The Report and Accounts shows him holding only 2,000 shares. His family trust holds 235,000. As he is not a trustee or beneficiary of this trust there is no obligation to disclose this holding.
> ■ J.F. Insch, a director of Guest Keen & Nettlefold's. He is shown as holding 4,166 shares. In 1970 he gave his children, none of whom were minors, 6,384 shares. These holdings do not need to be disclosed.

It may be possible to find family, trust etc. shareholdings in the list of shareholders (in the file at Companies House). However there are difficulties here: for example GKN has over 60,000 shareholders. But look at the directors' names in the list of shareholders, as it might disclose a holding by a wife, unmarried sister or children.

### Number of employees:

The company is obliged to give the average number of employees in the UK 'under contracts of service' in each week and their remuneration (pay). In arriving at the figure, the company adds together the number of employees in each week and divides by fifty-two. This is a poor guide to the size of the work force and its pay: if a lot of workers are sacked at the end of the year, this will not come out clearly in the figure.

If the company employs a lot of part-time workers the figure will be a very inaccurate guide to the average level of pay. The phrase 'under contracts of service' excludes lump labour, temporary workers and workers supplied by employment agencies. The pay figure includes overtime and directors' pay.

Wholly-owned subsidiaries of UK companies do not have to provide the information at all.

There is no obligation to show the number of workers overseas – though some companies do this.

Sometimes a clue to the employment trend abroad is the share of turnover overseas, from year to year. Also some companies give a breakdown of capital expenditure for the UK and overseas. This can help.

> ■ The 1971 Report of Carrington Viyella shows that sales from companies overseas accounted for 7½ per cent of total group sales, but nearly 30 per cent of new capital expenditure (spending on new plant) was going abroad. During 1971, the company's labour force in the UK fell from 37,000 to 31,500. Abroad it increased from 1,200 to 1,500.

Despite these problems, this is often the only figure that gives a clue to the average weekly wage in a company.

### Chairman's statement:

In addition to the Directors' Report there may be the Chairman's statement.

The Chairman's statement will sometimes provide useful information, but remember that the company has secrets which it wants to keep from competitors, customers, suppliers, possible bidders, the government and the workers. Therefore it may play down the importance of one side of the business or its profitability.

> ■ Watney's 1971 Report and Accounts mentioned their club service – a system by which workingmen's clubs, British Legion clubs etc., have finance and drink provided by the brewery. This was the first time it was mentioned in a Report, even though it was a well-established practice that had been going on for years.
>
> ■ When Reo Starkis floated his hotel company in 1972, Scottish and Newcastle Breweries appeared as a substantial backer. There had never been any mention of it in the S&N Report and Accounts in previous years.

These examples illustrate how misleading Chairmen's statements can be by omission – presumably in an attempt to keep competitors ignorant: some of the hotels using Scottish and Newcastle products might have been less keen to do so, if they had known that Scottish and Newcastle was backing one of their competitors.

There is obviously a limit to what the Chairman can hide and to how misleading he can be. Remember he wants to portray the company in the best light to his shareholders – often that means saying that productivity has increased, the labour force reduced, etc. Look out for phrases like 'adjusting the work load', 'economies in the handling of business'. (Thanks to the Guardian Royal Exchange Assurance for these.)

A reading of Chairmen's statements over the last few years should give some indication of what has been happening: it is surprising how many times Chairmen's statements contrast oddly with later events.

■ Carrington Viyella's 1971 Report and Accounts published in March 1972:
'*A high level of activity was maintained throughout the year by Gainsborough Cornard Ltd.*' October 1972: Planned closure of Gainsborough Cornard factory in Great Yarmouth – 340 redundancies.

# 10.

## The Profit and Loss Account

This chapter explains the terms used in Profit and Loss Accounts.

The **Profit and Loss Account** will look something like the example on page 45. Some of the entries will have numbers by them, indicating that notes to the entries appear in the Notes to the Profit and Loss Account. These Notes give extra information, and should be treated as part of the Profit and Loss Account.

A complete list of the information that companies are required to show in the Profit and Loss Account is shown in Appendix 2. Here are the most important items:

■ Turnover, and how it is arrived at.
■ Income from rents, if a substantial part of the company's revenue.
■ Income from quoted and unquoted investments.
■ Directors' emoluments (pay) and pay of the Chairman. Details of number of employees who receive more than £10,000 a year.
■ Auditor's remuneration.
■ Cost of hiring plant and machinery.
■ Amount provided for depreciation, and how it is calculated.
■ Tax paid.
■ Dividends paid and proposed.
■ Transfers to and from reserves.
■ Any exceptional factors affecting the Profit and Loss Account and any change in accounting practices.

# The purpose of the Profit and Loss Account:

The law requires the Profit and Loss Account to give a 'true and fair view' of the profit and loss of the company for the financial year. This phrase is often quoted in the Auditors' Report, which must accompany the Accounts. The Auditors' Report sometimes also includes the phrase 'as concerns the member of the company'. This is important. (Members here means shareholders.)

To present a 'fair view' to the shareholders various assumptions are made. These assumptions understate the size of the surplus produced by labour.

The Profit and Loss Account does not show the amount of money the company will have in the bank at the end of that year. The Balance Sheet of a company represents the wealth of the company, and how it has paid for it: the value of the factories and stocks. The Profit and Loss Account shows how much these assets earn for their owners. The money left, after paying wages, tax and dividends, stays in the company to increase the assets that appear in the Balance Sheet. The Profit and Loss Account can be used to discover the surplus the workers are producing. The Balance Sheet represents the accumulation of the surplus.

# How profit is calculated:

The arrangement of individual Profit and Loss Accounts varies enormously. This doesn't mean that some companies escape giving the information required by law, but just that it is shown in a different place.

**Pre-tax profit** is the profit that is liable for tax, after crediting items of income and deducting costs. As companies vary in their presentation, using different headings and putting information in unusual places, here is a table showing how the pretax profit is arrived at.

| | |
|---|---|
| Receipts from sales (turnover) | 100,000 |
| Deduct: Cost of all raw materials | 30,000* |
| Deduct: Cost of labour | 30,000 |
| Deduct: Other overheads | 10,000* |
| Trading profits | 30,000 |
| Deduct: Depreciation | 5,000 |
| Deduct: Interest | 5,000 |
| Pretax profit | 20,000 |

This is how the company arrives at the pre-tax figure. The company has no obligation to give those two items marked with an asterisk, although some of the other overheads are given.

**Turnover:**

Turnover means sales. The figure is the total value of sales the company makes.

Many companies are vertically integrated. They don't just manufacture (say) cars, they also make the parts that are used in the cars. If the sales of those subsidiary companies that make the parts were included in the total sales figure, it would give a very misleading view of the sales of the company as a whole. The Notes to the Profit and Loss Account should always make reference to the fact that inter-company sales have been excluded.

■The 1971 Report and Accounts of the British Oxygen Company contains the note: 'Sales are based on invoiced value excluding inter-company sales.'

Invoiced value means the figure that appeared on the invoice (i.e. the notification of delivery, with the prices) they sent out to their customers. Sales do not include orders received but not yet delivered. Sales do not represent money that has been received for goods.

There is no statutory requirement to show the geographical spread of sales; only the total value of exports. The Stock Exchange recommends that the company gives a geographical breakdown of sales. This is only a recommendation. Not all companies follow it.

### Investment and rental income:

Income from rents and investments is self-explanatory. For most companies this is fairly small: but not always. Distillers has an enormous stake in British Petroleum; Whitbreads have many shareholdings in small brewers. Such shareholdings can arise for a variety of reasons: Distillers sold a company to BP in exchange for BP shares.

Investment income represents the dividends of interest from these shareholdings. In some cases it is very important:

> ■British and Commonwealth Shipping Company's investment income pays for the dividend payments to shareholders. Such investment income comes to the company regardless of the trading background for the company and without the company having to do anything.

The company has to distinguish between **unquoted** and **quoted** investment income. Quoted companies are those whose shares are dealt in on a Stock Exchange.

The larger the amount of investment income, the less vulnerable is the company to its own workforce; less committed to its productive activities.

### Remember:

The money that is invested is the accumulation of years of surplus. The income from it is a target in bargaining.

### Directors' pay and allowances:

The directors' fees should be shown in a table in ranges of £2,500. There is no list of how much each director is paid – though if any director has a service agreement, the figure will be found there. Service agreements can be inspected at the company's office. The amount paid to the Chairman is shown separately.

The total amount received by the directors must be shown –
salaries and any commission related to sales or any other for-
mula. Any pensions to directors and compensation payments
also have to be shown.

> ■ In the 1972 accounts of insurance brokers C.T. Bowring,
> it was revealed that the company had paid pension
> contributions for the 14 directors of £119,000. This was
> in addition to profit commission of £263,000.

There is no requirement to show payment in kind and although loans to directors must be shown, there is no obligation to show if the director is living in a house owned by the
company. Sometimes (mainly in private companies) the non-
monetary benefits directors receive are shown, so look in the
Notes carefully.

> ■ Bredero–Price, an extremely profitable Dutch–American
> owned North Sea Gas pipe-coating operation, shows in
> its 1971 accounts £9,085 spent on directors' and executives'
> travelling and entertainment, compared with £8,830 spent
> on safety measures for the labour force.
> ■ A. & P. Appledore International, a company owned
> jointly by Court Line, then still in business, and London
> Overseas Freighters, made £85,000 pre-tax in 1972, after
> £35,000 directors' fees and £7,700 travelling and entertain-
> ment expenses.

One of the perks of being a director is being able to eat
expense account meals. It is impossible to tell from the
accounts how much these fringe benefits are worth.

The taxman does not recognize expense account meals as a
tax deductible expense unless they are in entertaining export
customers. The way such expenses are treated in the accounts
is to hide them in the tax figure. There are two ways in which
this can be done. The company will show pre-tax profits after
charging these non-deductible items; then it will: *either* have a
tax charge slightly above the standard rate, because it will
include tax on higher profits than in the pre-tax figure; *or*
the company will show a standard tax charge and the tax due
on non-deductible expenses will be taken off the transfer to
the deferred taxation or tax equalization account.

### Auditor's remuneration:

This is the amount paid to the firm of accountants who
have prepared the Report and Accounts.

### Hired plant and machinery:

If a company is hiring all its machinery it will appear from the Balance Sheet that it owns no machinery at all, but is nonetheless making profits. The amount being paid out in hire charges is important to the worker: an employer who is hiring his machinery will be less likely to keep on labour if business gets difficult. A hire agreement comes to an end or can be terminated much more quickly than a whole factory and its contents can be sold. This is the attraction to the businessman: he is less tied down to one particular line of business and he can make profits from a much smaller outlay.

### Exceptional items:

The company has to reveal any unusual, exceptional or non-recurring items and details of any change in the basis of accounting. These are often in the Notes. They may occur either before or after pre-tax profits.

Exceptional items can be very important: they often cover closure costs (including redundancy payments) and losses or profits on the disposal of fixed assets.

> ■ Wiggins Teape 1971 accounts showed a profit of £1.08 million, but after £10 million worth of repairs, renewals and obsolescence write-offs.

### Exceptional items are important because:

■ They can reduce apparent profits in one year on a non-recurring basis.
■ They can be a clue to the degree of rationalization going on.
■ They may signify a profit breakthrough in later years as a result of these measures.

### Depreciation:

This figure is very important and can be very misleading. It is the source of much of the manipulation of the profit figure that appears in the accounts.

Expenses are incurred in the running of the company: wages, raw materials, overheads. Another cost is the purchase of plant and machinery. When these items come to the end of their life they will be sold and will not be worth as much as they cost. Firms want to spread the cost of the machinery over its useful life. Provision is made for this decrease in value, for its depreciation.

This provision, which is deducted from profits before they are assessed for tax, represents cash retained in the business, available for investment in plant and machinery to replace the plant which has been scrapped.

> ■ A company buys a machine for £100. It expects that machine to last nine years and to be worth £10 at the end of that time. There are two methods of depreciation the company can use:
> 1. The company writes off (depreciates) £10 a year for each of the nine years of the machine's life. This method of depreciation is called the *straight line method.*
> 2. Or the company can use the *reducing balance* method. In this the company writes off a fixed percentage each year and, as the (written down) value is lower each year, the actual amount of depreciation is reducing all the time.

The two systems are explained more fully on pages 159–160. The system used and the assumption made about the life of the machine and its value at the end of its life have a big impact on profits. The reducing balance method will make profits appear lower in the early part of a machine's life than the straight line method.

**Companies will normally say which system of depreciation they use.** The most commonly used is the straight line method.

The depreciation figure given in the Accounts is arrived at by using either of these systems for every piece of equipment the company owns. It is also applied to short leasehold property. Some companies also depreciate freehold property.

> ■ By 1972 Barclays Bank had accumulated depreciation of £19 million. £9 million of this was on freehold property. In most companies' accounts that £9 million would have been shown as profit.

In recent years, when property appreciated in value, most companies stopped depreciating freehold property. But if a company does still do this, add that part of the depreciation charge to pretax profits to arrive at the real profit figure. Depreciating freehold property is just another way of hiding profits in the Balance Sheet.

Some companies, which have not revalued their property at all, still have it in the accounts after depreciation applied years ago (see page 161).

Another anomaly is the depreciation of ships, many of which last much longer than the period over which they are written off and in some cases actually increase in value as the demand for their services increases.

# Inflation accounting:

This is another way in which companies can reduce their published profits. The theory behind inflation accounting is that in a period of rising prices the value of a £ of profit is less at the end of the year than it was at the beginning. Company accounts, which are compiled from factual documents, ignore this and as a result there are three ways in which the Report and Accounts do not give a true record of a company's profitability.

■ There is no way of distinguishing between profits made from the increased value of stock because of rising prices and profits made from normal trading.

■ The cost of new machinery is rising, so the fund for replacement that is built up through depreciation based on cost is clearly inadequate.

■ No account is taken of the loss of purchasing power of any cash the company owned during a period of rapid inflation. Similarly, there is no record of the benefit companies get from borrowing at a fixed rate of interest. £1 million borrowed ten years ago is worth much less than it was then, so a company which borrowed this amount benefited at the expense of whoever lent it.

Although the various professional bodies are still arguing about the system of inflation accounting that should be used, all the systems aim to show a company's profits in terms of the value of the £ at the end of its accounting period.

The most widely used system of inflation accounting is the Current Purchasing Power approach. The method is quite simple. Using the Retail Price Index – or some other measure of prices – all the company's non-monetary assets (stock, land, equipment) are increased in value by the percentage increase in the index between the date when they were bought and the year end.

As a result:

■ the cost of beginning of year stock is increased, and so profits fall;

■ the value of fixed assets rises, so the depreciation charge rises and profits fall.

The same system is applied to all monetary assets – cash owned, debtors and creditors. The value of these is reduced by the increase in the Retail Price Index as they have lost that much buying power. As a result, profits of companies owning a lot of cash and owed money are reduced.

■ In 1973 the profits of property companies as measured by inflation accounting were 310 per cent higher than appeared from their books because of the high level of their long term borrowing and ownership of property.

Brewers and hotel companies' profits were 38 per cent higher because of the high level of their borrowing and because their assets (and therefore depreciation charges) are low relative to the level of profits.

Store companies' profits were 5 per cent higher because they are financed by their suppliers: they owe a lot of money.

Textile and engineering companies' profits were nearly 50 per cent lower because they carry a high level of stocks (so profits contain a high element of stock profit) and because profits are low relative to fixed assets, so the depreciation charge bites heavily into profits.

(See *Accounting for Inflation: Recent Proposals and their Effect* by P.W. Parker and P.M.D. Gibbs, published by the Institute of Actuaries, April 1974.)

Workers can ignore the adjustment of monetary assets for inflation. This is just a technique for identifying which capitalist organizations benefit from inflation and which lose. The 'gain' to profits a company makes by borrowing money is a loss to someone elsewhere in the system – the lender. The profits lost re-surface elsewhere in the system.

The adjustment for stock profits and depreciation is more important.

### Stock profits:

Imagine a man who has a vegetable stall in a market. He buys cabbages for 6p and sells them for 10p. But before he sells them all, the farmer increases the price of cabbages to 8p and the market price rises to 12p. If the stallholder who had bought his at 6p sells them for 12p, 2p of his profit is a stock profit. The profit has arisen because he was holding stocks before the price rise. But to replace his stocks he will have to pay 8p, so his 'real profit' is still only 4p.

Inflation accounting aims to eliminate such stock profits, so that companies' profits are shown after they have made provision for replacing the stock. The American method of stock valuation, 'last in-first out' (see page 157) automatically does this.

As no company uses inflation accounting in the main Profit and Loss Account, this means that almost all British company accounts contain some element of stock profits.

One exception is Tate & Lyle which uses a 'base stock' valuation method. The effect of this is to ensure any profit made from the rising value of sugar is kept out of the Profit and Loss Account.

## Depreciation:

Suppose you buy a car for £500 and decide that you will replace it in five years' time. If you save £100 a year, you will not have enough money to replace the car at the end of the five-year period, because of price rises. This is the exact position of companies that calculate their depreciation on the historic cost of machinery rather than replacement cost. As nearly all companies calculate depreciation on historic costs, profits are overstated to the extent that one cost of running the business is understated in the Profit and Loss Account.

The main reason most companies are anxious to introduce inflation accounting in a period of rising prices is to persuade the government that they are not making sufficient profit to finance investment and should therefore pay less tax.

Managements are likely to use the same arguments with the unions: 'It has been argued that inflation accounting could be valuable in convincing the trade unions that companies were not making excessive profits and that there must be restraint in pressing for wage increases.' (See *Accounting for Inflation* by P.W.Parker and P.M.D. Gibbs.)

If workers forego wage increases it will only increase the profits of the company, whether before or after inflation accounting. Workers have no control over those profits or their use and no guarantee that they will benefit from the improved financial strength that comes from making proper allowance for inflation. There is no indication that companies are going to stop paying dividends because of inflation accounting. There can be no question of workers sacrificing wages for companies to pay out dividends.

### What should be the workers' attitude to inflation accounting?

By agreeing to inflation accounting you strengthen a company without any guarantee that you will benefit from that strengthening.

Stock profits are real money – they are capital gains that the company makes. In the example of the vegetable stall-holder it is the customer who pays his stock profit. The ability to pass on his extra costs greatly improves his financial position. If companies could not benefit from rising prices in this way, they would be in as weak a position as the worker who cannot protect himself against rising prices.

By eliminating stock profits no account is taken of the strategic power companies have to restrict supplies, thus forcing up prices, once they have ensured they have plenty of stocks at the lower prices.

The position of a company that owns machinery is similar to that of someone who owns a house. Suppose you bought a house for £5,000 ten years ago. If you sell it for £10,000 you will have made a 'profit' of £5,000, but all of that will be needed to buy a replacement house of the same standard. The very forces that enabled you to make that profit ensure that the house you are buying has risen in price in the same way as the house you have just sold. But if you are just a tenant, assuming there is no rent control, at the end of ten years you have the same house, which you don't own, but you are paying much more rent.

Companies that own plant and machinery, although faced with rising costs to replace it, have the consolation that the value of the old machinery is not falling as fast as it would if replacement prices remained stable. The capital value of old machinery makes a useful contribution to the cost of replacing it.

The effect is also moderated by improving productivity – the replacement machine may cost more in money terms, but as it is capable of producing more, more quickly, the real increase is much lower.

The government also helps. As explained on pp. 110–11, the system of capital allowances allows companies to write off the cost of machines over a very short period of time, so that an extra source of funds for replacement is the deferred taxation account.

Companies that retain a high proportion of profits are effectively making allowance for the rising cost of replacing machinery. The effect of replacement cost depreciation is to reduce pre tax (and therefore after-tax) profits, but increase depreciation. As a company's funds for future investment comprise depreciation plus profits after dividends, the redistribution of money from one of these to another makes no difference to the wealth of the company, although it affects the figure in the Profit and Loss Account.

The impact of adjusting accounts for inflation can be dramatic:

■ Excluding stock profits and calculating depreciation on the basis of replacement cost, British Leyland's profits in 1973 were not £51.3 million but minus £24.6 million.

**The question workers must ask is: where did this profit go?**

The answer is that it is retained in the business, even though it is not called profit. The effect of inflation accounting is to make the company much stronger financially. But this wealth does not belong to the workers. **Inflation accounting can only be accepted on condition that:**

■ Wages are guaranteed to be inflation proof.

■ The benefits of inflation accounting are shared by workers.

The only complete and just answer can be the socialization of corporate wealth under workers' control.

# Tax charges and tax paid:

The figure given for depreciation is an expense of running the business, but it is not money that actually leaves the business in the way that wages do. The depreciation figure shown in the Report and Accounts is not the same as that recognized by the taxman in deciding the figure upon which to charge tax. Although the company may, for its own internal purposes and for the Profit and Loss Account, charge a 20 per cent rate of depreciation, the taxman treats it differently. He allows a higher rate of depreciation. This can be established by looking at the tax figure.

The Profit and Loss Account in the diagram on page 45 shows a tax charge of £5,665,000. In fact this company only paid £3,985,000 in tax. The reason is that the government allows much higher rates of depreciation than the company charges. These government allowances are called *Capital Allowances*.

The government is normally anxious to promote investment, and so it allows companies to write off as an expense of production a very large part of the cost of plant and machinery in the first year of ownership. These write-offs are made before tax. For the period 20 July 1971 to 31 July 1973 companies were allowed to write off 80 per cent of the cost, before being assessed for tax. Now it is 100 per cent in the first year.

So:

**If a company spends £100 on a machine,** it is immediately allowed £100 of profit tax-free. Pages 132–33 explain what happens to the tax that is shown in the Profit and Loss Account that is not paid to the taxman.

This system of encouraging investment replaced a system of investment grants, which were cash gifts to the company (see Chapter 14.)

Imagine a company continually investing in plant and machinery and buying expensive machinery. It is quite possible that in every year 100 per cent of the cost will exceed the pretax profit. In that case, the company will not pay any tax at all. But it will still show a tax charge in the Profit and Loss Account.

Some companies are even better off than this: ships, capital equipment for scientific research and immobile plant and machinery in development areas have a system of 'free depreciation'. This means the company can write off the cost of assets as it likes and usually it writes off the total cost in the first year. Because ships are expensive, but the profits generated comparatively small, most shipping companies never pay tax.

> ■ European Ferries. Between 1970 and 1973 the company made profits of £18.4 million, on which it paid tax of £624,000. On 31 December 1973 it still had £14 million of capital allowances available to set against future profits. The directors said: 'Under present legislation, no material liability is anticipated in the foreseeable future.'

Most companies hide the tax that they don't pay in a *tax equalization charge or deferred taxation account*. The company assumes a full tax charge, and this appears in the Profit and Loss Account. The share of this tax which isn't paid (because the taxman allows a higher level of depreciation than the company uses) is transferred to a tax equalization or deferred tax account in the Balance Sheet. The Notes to the Accounts will show the amount of tax that has been accumulated in the tax equalization account. The Notes should distinguish between tax that has been deferred because of the system of capital allowances and tax which is to be paid at a specified date in the future. The system is explained more fully, with an illustration of how it works, on pages 132–33.

In theory the tax equalization account is money that will eventually be paid to the taxman. In practice it is not.

**As most companies are continually reinvesting they never pay a full tax charge.**

> ■ In 1972 Courtaulds said that the £23 million that it had provided for eventual payment of this tax would clearly never be paid and so reduced the tax bill by the relevant amount. Courtaulds' 1973 Profit and Loss Account showed a tax bill of 15 per cent of profits.

Claims by management that the tax equalization account represents money owed to the taxman should be treated with scepticism: Courtaulds gave that money to the shareholders. They did not give it to the workers.

Tax provided for in the Profit and Loss Account but not paid is transferred to either a tax equalization account or to deferred taxation. This information should be in a Note to the Accounts.

### Standard tax rate:

In April 1973 the UK changed to a system of company taxation, called the imputation system. Most of the Reports and Accounts published up to the end of 1973, will have shown the old system of taxation. This is how it worked:

The government taxed companies at 40 per cent; most companies simply apply a 40 per cent tax charge to the pre-tax profit, i.e. after charging depreciation and interest.

Tax is charged for the financial year 1 April to 31 March. Many companies' accounting periods don't coincide with the government's financial year, so at the end of the company's year, tax is often owed to the taxman. Tax is paid nine months after the end of the (government's) financial year in which the company's accounting period ends.

■ If a company's year ended on 31 December 1972, tax would be payable December 1973 – i.e. 9 months after 31 March 1973.

The company normally charges the standard tax charge against its profits and transfers the tax which is to be paid on a later date to its Balance Sheet either as a current liability or, possibly, as part of deferred taxation.

The tax bill may differ from the standard rate for three reasons:

■ **Overseas tax:**

Many foreign countries have different (often higher) tax rates than the U.K.

■ **Tax losses:**

If a company loses (say) £1,000 in one year, then in future the first £1,000 of profit made is tax free. These tax losses can sometimes be substantial and the company is obliged to refer to any special circumstances affecting the tax figure in that or any succeeding year, in the accounts.

■ The company does not employ a tax equalization charge.

Although taxation laws now lay down strict conditions governing tax losses, it can still be worthwhile for a company to buy another company with tax losses, to reduce its own tax bill.

### Imputation tax:

This is the system of taxation introduced in April 1973. The diagram below illustrates how it works.

**Company tax: Imputation and Corporation Tax**

| | Imputation tax | | Corporation tax |
|---|---|---|---|
| Pretax profit | 2000 | Pretax profit | 2000 |
| Tax @ 52% | 1040 | Tax @ 40% | 800 |
| | | | 1200 |
| But the company pays dividends of: | 700 | Dividend | 1045 (before tax @ 33%) |
| | | Retained profit | 155 |
| So, company is allowed 33/67 of this as ACT relief: | 345 | | |
| So, tax paid | 1040–345 | | |
| | = 695 | | |
| So, profit: | 2000 | | |
| Less tax: | 695 | | |
| | 1305 | | |
| Less dividend | 700 | | |
| | 605 | | |
| ACT paid | 345 | | |
| Retained profit: | 260 | | |

In column A the company makes a pretax profit of £2,000. It pays tax at the new rate of 52 per cent. (The rate can be varied by the government.) But it also pays dividends of £700. These are paid tax-free to the shareholder, so the company is allowed to credit the tax that it has had to pay on the shareholders' behalf. This credit is called the Advance Corporation Tax (ACT) relief. It is equal to 33/67ths of the dividend; the reason for this rather odd amount is that income tax is 33 per cent. The ACT credit equals the tax paid on the dividend. (The shareholder gets a certificate to say that the company has paid the tax on his behalf.) So the company's tax bill is shown in line 5: the 52 per cent charge, less the ACT relief.

Lines 6 to 10 show what happens: the company pays its £695 of tax, pays the dividends and pays the shareholders' tax (line 10). The result is that the company is left with £260. Column B shows how the old system worked. The new system means that the shareholder can still receive the same dividend after tax and the company is better off. Only the taxman loses.

An important feature of this new system is that if the government increases tax on dividends it is still possible for the shareholder to receive exactly the same dividend. Suppose the government were to increase the tax rate on dividends to 50 per cent, instead of 33 per cent. This is how the sum would look:

| | |
|---|---|
| Pretax profit | 2000 |
| Tax @ 52 per cent | 1040 |
| Company pays net dividend of: | 700 |
| Assume 50 per cent rate on dividend, so ACT relief is 50/50 | 700 |
| So, the company pays | 1040–700 |
| | = 340 tax |
| Company pays tax on dividend | 700 |
| Company retains | 260 |

What happens is that the company's tax bill is reduced to pay the shareholders' tax. There is no increase in revenue for the taxman. The only way to increase the tax revenue is to increase corporation tax as well.

### Minority interests:

Sometimes a company, instead of owning all the share capital of another company, owns between 50 and 100 per cent. Suppose Company A owns 75 per cent of Company B. Because B is controlled by A, it is a subsidiary, and all its profits are brought into the A accounts. But in working out the profit attributable to the shareholders of A, the share of the profit that is attributable to the holders of 25 per cent of B has to be taken out. This is the deduction for the minority interest.

### Associated companies:
Sometimes there will be reference to the profit attributable to associated companies. There is no statutory obligation to show this but it is a recommendation of the Institute of Chartered Accountants and so is being increasingly followed.

An associated company is one where another company owns at least 20 per cent, but not more than 50 per cent of the share capital.

If Company A owns 20 per cent of Company B, then 20 per cent of B's profit would come into A's pre-tax figure. It follows there is no deduction at the minority level.

### Profit attributable to shareholders:
**This is the profit, after the tax has been paid and the minority interests deducted, that can be paid out in dividends to the shareholders.**

The Companies Acts require a company to show the share of this profit that is attributable to the parent company, and often in the Profit and Loss Account it will say 'of which £ ... has been dealt with in the accounts of the parent company.' This information can sometimes be helpful in building up a picture of where in the company the profits are made.

### Dividends:
This is the share of profits paid to shareholders. Although dividends are related to the profits of the company there is no obligation to pay the profits out in dividends. At the moment the government restrict the amount by which dividends can be increased.

The pre-tax figure is a part-measure of the surplus produced by the workers; the dividends are the share of that surplus paid to the shareholders in any one year.

**But remember:**

Money not paid out in dividends stays in the company to produce higher profits in future years. This makes the shareholders richer. This expected increase in profits will probably be reflected in the increased value of the company's shares. When the City values shares, it concentrates on profit per share, not dividend per share. The profit investors make on the increased value of their shares is taxed at a maximum of 30 per cent, which is below the minimum tax rate on dividends. So dividends paid are not a measure of a company's wealth, the size of labour's surplus or the return that a shareholder may receive on his investment.

But sometimes a company will pay dividends even when it is not making profits, by borrowing from the bank. There are several reasons why companies might do this:

■ It pleases the shareholders and therefore discourages them from criticizing the board.

■ The directors have confidence in the future: the dividends are usually paid well after the end of a company's financial year.

■ The directors may just be trying to give the impression that all is well. A company will want to do this as the ease with which it can get credit and bank loans is related to its suppliers' view of the company's stability.

To maintain trustee status (some investment funds are restricted to investing in trustee stocks), a company must have a continuous dividend record. So, sometimes a nominal dividend will be paid.

**Balance carried forward:**

This is what is left in the company after the dividends have been paid; it becomes part of the company's wealth, recorded in the Balance Sheet.

# II.

# The Balance Sheet

This chapter is divided into three parts:
1. The purpose of the Balance Sheet.
2. The Financing (or Capital Employed) side of the Balance Sheet.
3. The assets (or Employment of capital) side of the Balance Sheet.

## The purpose of the Balance Sheet:

The Balance Sheet shows the wealth of the company. It will look something like the Balance Sheet on page 118.

A Balance Sheet has two 'sides'. These two sides are not always printed side by side; sometimes they are printed (as illustrated here) one above the other.

One side shows the assets of the company, the other side shows how these assets have been financed.

The **Capital Employed side** shows the money put up by the shareholders and the accumulation of retained profits over the years. The **Employment of Capital side** shows how this money has been spent. (The two sides are sometimes headed, respectively, 'Financed By' and 'Assets Employed'.)

Both sides of the Balance Sheet must have the same total: the assets of the business cannot be worth more than the total amount of money put into the business. Some assets rise in value without any more money being put into them, particularly property and Stock Exchange investments. If the directors decide to increase the value of these assets in the Balance Sheet, they need to put an entry on both sides. There will be a reference in either the Balance Sheet or the

**ENGLISH CALICO LIMITED**

# Group Balance Sheet at 3rd February 1973

|  | 1973 £,000 |  | 1972 £,000 |
|---|---|---|---|
| **EMPLOYMENT OF CAPITAL** | | | |
| Fixed assets | | 45,940 | 44,541 |
| Investments | | 2,129 | 1,486 |
| | | 48,069 | 46,027 |
| **Current assets** | | | |
| Stocks | 47,321 | | 45,966 |
| Debtors | 29,555 | | 26,273 |
| Short-term loans, bank and cash balances | 4,625 | | 1,381 |
| | 81,501 | | 73,620 |
| **Current liabilities** | | | |
| Creditors | 19,413 | | 17,279 |
| Taxation | 4,143 | | 3,233 |
| Short-term borrowings | 9,475 | | 11,264 |
| Preference dividend | 98 | | 98 |
| Ordinary dividends—interim and proposed final | 2,926 | | 2,054 |
| | 36,055 | | 33,928 |
| **Net current assets** | | 45,446 | 39,692 |
| | | 93,515 | 85,719 |
| **Deferred liabilities** | | | |
| Provision for past service pensions | 4,077 | | 2,284 |
| Tax equalisation | 1,438 | 5,515 | 2,554 | 4,838 |
| | | 88,000 | 80,881 |
| **CAPITAL EMPLOYED** | | | |
| Ordinary share capital | | 34,236 | 34,236 |
| Reserves | | 24,298 | 17,347 |
| Ordinary shareholders' funds | | 58,534 | 51,583 |
| Preference share capital | | 5,880 | 5,880 |
| Minority interests | | 2,035 | 1,817 |
| Loan capital | | 21,551 | 21,601 |
| | | 88,000 | 80,881 |

Neville Butterworth
A. M. B. Kirsop       } Directors
T. Weatherby

Notes to a 'surplus on the revaluation of property'; on the Capital Employed side the increased value is frequently described in this way, under the 'Reserves' heading (see below).

The Employment of Capital side of the Balance Sheet usually has three main sub-headings: *fixed assets, current assets* and *current liabilities.*

Current assets and current liabilities are called 'current' because they are already, or are expected to become cash within one year of the publication of the Balance Sheet.

Current liabilities, therefore, include bank overdrafts, tax owed but not paid, and creditors (people to whom the company owes money). The bank and the company's suppliers are helping to finance the company's business, but as the finance is not long-term finance, they don't appear on the Capital Employed side of the Balance Sheet.

Some companies do put the current liabilities on the Capital Employed side. As can be seen from the diagram on page 118, this will not prevent the Balance Sheet from balancing: adding the £36,055,000 in current liabilities to £88,000,000 on the Capital Employed side gives £124,055,000, equal to fixed assets plus current assets, less deferred liabilities. This is an old-fashioned way of presenting the Balance Sheet but it is not uncommon in the accounts of private companies.

So the assets of a company exactly match its liabilities, giving the company no net value. This is correct: the company is not worth anything: all the wealth is attributable to the shareholders.

Page 179 shows you how to work out the wealth attributable to the shareholders, and page 150 gives examples of the returns some shareholders have received from their original investment.

The requirements of the Companies Acts are fairly detailed, so that much of the information required for the Balance Sheet will appear in Notes to the Balance Sheet. There should be reference to the appropriate Notes in the Balance Sheet itself.

# Capital Employed: the financing side of the Balance Sheet:

Details must be given of all the shares in issue, distinguishing between the different types of shares.

**Remember:**

■ Especially in the case of public companies, present shareholders will generally have no connexion with the shareholders who originally put up the money to start the business.

■ The value of a share is the price at which it can be sold on the Stock Market. This price is only indirectly related to the fortunes of the company.

**Ordinary shares:**

The ordinary shareholders are the owners of the company. This is often called the **equity** interest. If a company is financed only by equity money, in the first year of a company's life, the only entry on the Capital Employed side of the Balance Sheet is the number of shares in issue.

In the UK all shares have a **par** or **nominal value.** It is a requirement of the Companies Act that the capital of the company is divided into shares of a fixed amount. This par value can be misleading. It is not the same as the price of the share in the Stock Market, or even the price at which the share is issued. But when a dividend is declared as X per cent, it is as a percentage of the par value.

As the Balance Sheet is a money record of the value of the company, it shows the total par value of the shares. Where the shares are 25p shares, one million shares would be represented in the Balance Sheet by £250,000.

The accounts will show both the **authorized** and the **issued share capital.** The authorized capital is the share capital registered as the capital of the company and recorded in the Memorandum of Association. It can be increased with the approval of shareholders. The directors can issue shares up to the authorized capital without the approval of shareholders. However the Stock Exchange have their own regulations governing the acquisitions of other companies through issuing new shares. Sometimes shareholders' approval will be required even though the shares issued are within the total authorized capital, because the acquisition is large, in relation to the size of the company's assets or profits.

Shares are **fully paid.** This means that the shareholders have paid the full par value of the shares and cannot be called upon by the directors to subscribe any more money. It is very unusual to find partly paid shares except in share-incentive schemes or employees' shares (see page 93–94).

## Preference shares:

The difference between preference shares and ordinary shares is that the preference shares receive a fixed dividend each year and are not entitled to any share of the company's profits other than this. If the company is wound up, the preference shareholders will be repaid before the ordinary shareholders. Some preference shares are described as *cumulative*. This means that if the dividend isn't paid in one year, it will be carried forward until the next, and when eventually the company can pay preference dividends again all the dividends in arrears will be paid to the shareholders.

Preference dividends are fixed interest securities, but they differ from the fixed interest stocks (described below) in that the dividends are paid from after-tax profits.

Preference shares rarely carry the right to vote, but sometimes there are special rights attached to the preference shareholders, which can be checked from the company's Articles of Association, or, if the company is a public company, from the *Stock Exchange Year-book*, or Extel statistical cards.

These rights can sometimes be very important:

■ Alfred Herbert is one of the largest machine tool makers in the country. The trust deed of the preference shares laid down certain circumstances in which the company had to ask permission of the preference shareholders if it wanted to borrow more money. Those circumstances arose in 1974. The John James Group owned 27 per cent of the preference shares and said it would refuse permission. It was only persuaded to change its mind when the government-backed Finance Corporation for Industry offered to buy its preference shares for twice the price of the shares in the Stock Market. If John James had not been bought out, Alfred Herbert might have gone into liquidation, through lack of finance.

If a director, or someone you are investigating, has a large holding of preference shares, check on the exact rights of the preference shares, as some have particularly attractive terms.

■ Preference shares of the Manchester Ship Canal Company and of Lister and Company (a textile manufacturer) have preferential rights to the assets of the company in the event of the company being wound up. The rights of shareholders in the event of a winding up are fundamental rights that have a value even if there is no such intention; for instance, if the company was taken over, the bidder would have to buy out the special rights of the preference shareholders.

Any arrears of preference dividends must be noted in the Report and Accounts. If there are arrears it is an indication of the serious lack of profitability of the enterprise.

### Other shares:

There may be shares other than ordinary or preference shares – particularly deferred shares or non-voting shares.

Generally **deferred shares** are shares whose right to receive dividends is deferred until some date or event in the future. Nowadays the attraction of deferred shares is that they often give the shareholder the opportunity to share in the increased wealth and profitability of the company – if the share price rises, reflecting the ultimate right to dividends and profits – without receiving any highly taxed dividends.

Sometimes there are **non-voting shares,** often called 'A' shares. The idea of non-voting shares was to ensure that control of the company remained in a few hands – quite disproportionate to the number of shares owned. They were used often by families that wanted the tax advantages of being a public company without having to sacrifice management control. Non-voting shares are, in fact, illegal in the EEC and they are on the decline in the UK. In some cases the enfranchisement of non-voting shares will make the company vulnerable to a takeover bid as the board can no longer block a takeover they disagree with.

### Increasing the share capital:

Any change in the company's share capital during the year must be shown in the Report and Accounts. There are four main reasons why the share capital may be increased:

■ To make an acquisition

■ Under the terms of any options or concession rights, such as a share incentive scheme (see page 93) or a convertible loan stock (see page 127)

■ A scrip issue

■ A rights issue

To understand how these last two work, it is necessary first to describe the reserves figure.

### Reserves:

There are two main categories of reserves: the **revenue reserve** and the **capital reserve**.

The legal distinction between the two is that the capital reserves are not available for paying dividends. (See below.)

**Revenue** reserves are the sum of the retained profits over the years: page 116 drew attention to the last line of the Profit and Loss Account, where it often says 'Balance carried forward to reserves.'

The revenue reserve figure is built up from these. As companies are required to show any changes in reserves in the Accounts, it is possible to trace the addition of the retained profit to the reserves each year by referring to the Notes to the Balance Sheet.

**Capital** reserves include profits on the sale of fixed assets and increases in the value of a fixed asset.

There will often be reference to the **share premium account** (part of the capital reserves). Shares are very rarely issued at their par value, because the price at which they are issued is related to many factors, the most important of which is the profitability of the company. This could well justify a price per share higher than the nominal value. If shares are issued at a premium to the nominal value, this premium is recorded in the share premium account.

> ◼ If a company issued 200,000 shares valued at £1, when the nominal value was 25p, only £50,000 of nominal share capital would be issued, with £150,000 being credited to the share premium account.

Reserves may sometimes include **provisions** or **charges against reserves.** Sometimes the directors will provide for a possible reduction in the value of the company's assets. A common charge against reserves is a currency loss.

> ◼ In its 1972 Report and Accounts, Courtaulds charged £4½ million against reserves, this being a reduction in the value of the company's assets as a result of currency changes.

Reserves are not cash. Although they are represented on the other side of the Balance Sheet by assets, these assets will be in forms other than cash. The word reserve is used to mean 'kept back', being originally money kept back from the shareholders (retained profits). In this way reserves are part of shareholders' funds like the amount entered under share capital.

### Scrip issues:

Because they are shareholders' funds the **reserves** can be distributed by way of **scrip (capitalization, bonus) issues.** It is important to understand what happens when a company gives a scrip issue. Suppose the Balance Sheet looks like this:

| *Assets* | £ | *Financed by* | £ |
|---|---|---|---|
| Fixed Assets | 10,000 | Share capital | 5,000 |
| Net current assets | 10,000 | Revenue reserve | 15,000 |
| | 20,000 | | 20,000 |

The company could make a scrip issue of one new share for every old one, and the financed by (Capital Employed) of the Balance Sheet would look like this:

| | |
|---|---|
| Share capital | 10,000 |
| Reserves | 10,000 |
| | 20,000 |

As the revenue reserve belongs to the shareholders anyway, they are no better off than before the scrip issue. And although they possess twice as many shares, the price in the Stock Market will be adjusted so that their shareholdings are worth the same as before.

Scrip issues are made chiefly for book-keeping reasons, but:

▣ If the company pays the same dividend on the share capital as increased by scrip issue, then shareholders will be better off, as they are receiving more dividends. Where there has been a scrip issue this should always be checked.

▣ In practice scrip issues are only made when the directors are confident of the future, and so they can be taken as a sign of the directors' view of future profitability.

The real reasons for directors making a scrip issue are little better than public relations:

▣ Half the shares of public companies are held by individuals. Many of these investors are unsophisticated. They think they are better off when they receive a scrip issue. This helps increase their loyalty to the board so that the directors are less likely to come under pressure from their shareholders and more likely to get their support if it is ever needed.

▣ It may increase the attractions of the company's shares. There is some prejudice on the Stock Market against share prices that are very high, for instance £8 rather than 80p. By making a scrip issue the directors will increase the number of shares in issue and reduce the price at which they are quoted.

### Rights issues:

The other way new shares may be issued to existing shareholders is by a rights issue. This is when a company gives existing shareholders the right to buy new shares, in proportion to their existing holding, at a price generally below the market price of the shares.

Under the old system of Corporation Tax (when companies 'paid' 40 per cent of their profits as tax) it was often considered a bad sign for a company to raise money by a rights issue:

■ It used to be thought that a rights issue showed the company needed more money than it could possibly provide from its own internal growth or obtain from its bank. This prejudice still remains and a rights issue can be a sign of cash problems in a company.

■ Rights issues can make the shareholders poorer. As there are more shares, the company has to earn much more profit just to maintain the same level of profit per share. Of course, because of the rights issue, it has more cash to help it earn these profits.

**Rights issues do offer something for nothing: shareholders are being offered shares at a lower price than non-shareholders would have to pay.**

## Loan capital:

The amount of **loan capital** a company has is important to the worker. Loan capital is money which has been lent to the company for a fixed period of time at a fixed price (rate of interest). The interest is paid by the company before it pays tax. As generally there are penalties to the company if the interest is not paid it is an expense that has to be met whatever the level of profitability.

**Bank overdrafts** do not appear as loan capital unless they have been negotiated for a fixed period of time, longer than one year.

Companies are required to show – which they normally do in the Notes to the Report and Accounts – the different types of loans, the date on which the original capital is redeemed (that is, the date the money is paid back) and the rate of interest paid. There are two main types of loan: **debentures and unsecured loans.**

In practice the important difference between the two is that a **debenture** is secured against assets of the company: in this way it is like a mortgage on a house. So if the company goes bankrupt the debenture holders will be paid back from the sale of some of the company's assets. They will be paid before settlement of debts to the company's trade creditors (those people who are owed money for goods they have sold to the company).

■ In 1971 Rolls Royce went bust, with estimated debts of over £60 million, but the debenture holders were repaid in full, often years before they would otherwise have been repaid. The government came to the rescue of the shareholders, who got some money back. Workers still lost their jobs.

**Unsecured loan stock** has not the same security, but if the company goes bankrupt the holders of the loan stock are repaid before the company's creditors.

Some loan stocks are called **convertible loan stocks.** These are convertible into ordinary shares in the company at special times, on specified terms.

### Advantages of loan capital to the businessman:

Loan capital is one of the ways of financing a business: instead of issuing more shares to shareholders (a rights issue) or using shareholders' money through retained profits, the businessman can borrow money for a fixed price.

Since the early 1960s, and especially since 1964, loan capital has increased dramatically in importance as a source of capital for British companies. In 1969 long-term loans accounted for 20 per cent of the capital of UK quoted companies, against 13 per cent in 1963. This is because companies have realized that **long-term borrowing is generally cheaper than issuing shares**, for the following reasons:

### ■ Effects of inflation:

Suppose a company borrows £100,000 at 10 per cent for 20 years. For each of these 20 years the company will pay £10,000 of interest, and in the twentieth year it will repay the £100,000. If the rate of inflation is 10 per cent a year, the value of that £10,000 and £100,000 in 20 years will be much less – £1,486 and £14,864 respectively. In other words, at the end of 20 years it is as though the company had borrowed £14,864 instead of £100,000. If the company had raised money from the ordinary shareholders, the dividends would have risen with the profits, which will tend to reflect the rate of inflation.

### ■ Real cost:

Interest on loans is paid out of pre-tax profits. So, when Corporation Tax was 40 per cent, the after-tax cost of interest payments was 60 per cent of the pre-tax cost. In other words, it can be much cheaper for the shareholder if the company borrows long term fixed interest money.

*Illustration:*

| *Borrowing £100 at 10%* | | *Not borrowing anything* |
|---|---|---|
| Pre-interest profit | 110 | 110 |
| Interest | 10 | — |
| | 100 | 110 |
| Tax at 40% | 40 | 44 |
| Leaving | 60 | 66 |

As this illustration shows, the cost to the ordinary shareholder, because the interest for long-term money is paid before tax, is only 6 per cent, not the 10 per cent it appears to be.

Compare this with the cost of ordinary shares: although the dividend yield (the dividend expressed as a percentage of the value of the shares) may be below 5 per cent, because the dividends can be expected to rise, the eventual cost will be much greater than fixed interest borrowing.

### Gearing:

Financial gearing is the relationship between the money a company uses on which it has to pay a fixed return – fixed-interest borrowing – and the money it uses which belongs to the ordinary shareholders – shareholders' funds – on which it pays dividends, which can rise and fall.

The greater the amount of fixed-interest borrowing relative to shareholders' funds, the more highly-geared a company is. High gearing has certain advantages.

*Illustration:*

Here are the Profit and Loss Accounts of two similar companies; one borrows a much larger proportion of its funds than the other.

|  | Company A | Company B |
| --- | --- | --- |
| Pre-interest profit | £250 | £250 |
| Interest paid | £100 | £200 |
| Pre-tax profit | £150 | £50 |

Company B is more highly geared than Company A. It pays twice as much interest and pre-tax profits are much lower than A's, where borrowings are much lower.

BUT suppose the companies were to double their pre-interest profit. The Profit and Loss Accounts would look like this:

|  | Company A | Company B |
| --- | --- | --- |
| Pre-interest profit | £500 | £500 |
| Interest paid | £100 | £200 |
| Pre tax profit | £400 | £300 |

Company A has increased its pre tax profits from £150 to £400, a 166 per cent increase, even though trading profits have only increased by 100 per cent. But Company B has increased its pre tax profits from £50 to £300, a 500 per cent increase.

**In highly-geared companies, increases in pre-interest profits produce much bigger increases in pre-tax profits, because the money which is financing the business takes only a fixed proportion of the profits.**

**But highly-geared companies need stability of profits, to pay the interest charges. And if pre-interest profits fall, pre-tax profits will fall much more.**

**The disadvantages of fixed-interest borrowing:**

■ If the fixed-interest debt is secured against particular pieces of property, the company cannot sell the property without the permission of the debenture holders. This problem is frequently overcome by creating a **floating charge.** This means that the loan is secured against the assets of the company generally, not just against one specific building. But even this can be a restriction on the directors' freedom to sell parts of the business.

■ The payment of the interest is much more important than the payment of dividends to shareholders: one year, or perhaps more, can go by without the shareholders being paid dividends, and without the directors being threatened. But not one payment of interest on loan stock can be missed.

**This has important implications for the worker:**
■ **The company searches for stability of profits.**
■ **It increases the pressure to maximize profits.**

### Profits, stability and size:

Because of the regular annual commitments to pay interest, it is important for the businessman to ensure that profits flow in regularly. He will make efforts to involve himself in non-cyclical industries, areas with few strikes, non-unionized workers, and industries not needing a large work force.

Payment of the interest on bank overdrafts is usually just as important.

> ■ In May 1974, the Ronald Lyon Group encountered serious financial problems; there were many redundancies. The event that precipitated this was the company's inability to pay the bank interest on an overdraft.

Fixed-interest borrowing increases the pressure to maximize profits because:
■ Although the cost of issuing ordinary shares will probably be more expensive over a long period, it may be less in the first year. So a greater rate of profitability will have to be achieved to pay the interest than if money had been raised from shareholders.
■ The ordinary shareholders will expect some return for their investment even after the company has borrowed long-term money. The company has to pay both the interest on the fixed interest and dividends to shareholders.
■ As well as trying to make the existing business more profitable, the businessman will search for new investments with a higher return.

Of course companies have some choice about how highly-geared they become. A company will only gear up if it is confident about the future profitability and growth of its business. **But:** things can go wrong, so the borrowing becomes a burden.

Because of the Stock Market's lack of enthusiasm for rights issues, companies often have to borrow money even when they would prefer not to.

**This is how to test a company's reliance on fixed-interest borrowing:** Express the fixed-interest borrowing as a percentage of shareholders' funds (the issued ordinary share capital and reserves). This ratio is called the **company's gearing.**

To get a better idea of the importance of borrowing, preference shares and bank overdrafts (although bank overdrafts are meant to be short-term) can be added to long-term loans and the total expressed as a percentage of shareholders' funds. The higher the percentage figure, the more reliant the company is on fixed-interest borrowing, and the greater the pressure on the management to produce stability of profits.

In UK industry generally this pressure has been increasing over the years: in 1964 all fixed-interest borrowing, including preference shares and bank overdrafts, amounted to 34 per cent of shareholders' funds. In 1969 it was 48 per cent and is now probably over 50 per cent. If a company relies more on fixed-interest borrowing than industry generally, the pressure to maximize profits and achieve stability of profits will be greater.

The profitability and balance sheet of an individual sector of industry can be found out from *Business Monitor: Company Accounts*, published annually by the Department of Industry.

### Outside shareholders' interest in subsidiaries:

This represents the interest of minorities (see pp. 114–15). When a company owns over 50 per cent of the shares in another company, the second company is a subsidiary. All the assets of the second company appear on the assets side of the Balance Sheet, but as they don't all belong to the shareholders of the parent company, a separate item has to appear on the financing side of the Balance Sheet. This item is the outside shareholders' interest in subsidiaries.

### Deferred liabilities:

Deferred liabilities are the debts a company has which do not have to be paid within one year. The four main types are:

■ Taxes
■ Money owed for businesses which have been bought on a deferred payment basis
■ Some special loans
■ Pension liabilities

### Taxes:

This is the most important deferred liability. The system of capital allowances is explained on pages 110–11. **Deferred tax** represents the tax that has been charged in the Profit and Loss Account but not paid because the company had invested in new equipment. This tax can appear either as a liability on the Employment of Capital side or as a source of capital on the Capital Employed side of the Balance Sheet, when it will be called the **tax equalization account** or **deferred taxation.**

**Illustration A : Profits: the story told to the taxman, Year 1**

| *Taxman's accounts* | | *Shareholders' accounts* | |
|---|---|---|---|
| Trading profit after interest £100 | | Trading profit after interest | £100 |
| Capital allowance | £80 | Depreciation | £10 |
| Profit subject to tax | £20 | Profit subject to tax | £90 |
| Tax at 50% | £10 | Tax at 50% | £45 |
| Profit after tax | £10 | Profit after tax | £45 |

*In this example the company is making £100 profit and has spent £80 on a new machine. The taxman allows the company to deduct 100 per cent (£80) of this cost from its profit before he levies tax.*

*The company, in its Report and Accounts to shareholders, is employing a different system, depreciating its assets on a more even basis over a period of years (in this case on the straight line basis over 8 years), the £35 difference between the tax charged in the two accounts is the amount transferred to deferred taxation in the Balance Sheet in the shareholders' accounts.*

*In the second year of the machine's life the taxman's accounts are going to look something like this:*

**Illustration B: Profits: the story told to the taxman, Year 2**

| | |
|---|---|
| Profit | £100 |
| Capital allowance | — |
| Profit subject to tax | £100 |
| Tax at 50% | £50 |
| Profit after tax | £50 |

*The same trading profit has been assumed, so the shareholders' accounts will look exactly as in Illustration A. The tax will appear as £45 even though £50 was paid, the £5 being paid from deferred taxation provided for in the Balance Sheet.*

*The difference in profit between year one and year two in the taxman's account is entirely attributable to the system of capital allowances. The company does, of course, make £100 profit in year one; it is just that the tax is only levied on £20 of it.*

*The company does not wish to show such dramatic fluctuations in profits because:*

■ Fluctuating profits will disturb the share price; when the share price falls, the wealth of the shareholder falls, and therefore investors don't like fluctuating profits. Companies with an even profit record are more highly rated by the Stock Market.

In both illustrations A and B the tax in the deferred taxation account is actually paid by the company. In reality it rarely is. This is because companies are continually investing and carrying forward substantial tax allowances.

■ In 1962, Guest, Keen and Nettlefold's deferred tax stood at £7.95 million; in 1970 it was £12.3 million.

Even if it is paid eventually, the company will have benefitted. The deferred tax payments are paid well after they were granted: the government gives a company tax relief of, say, £100 now; but when the company pays it in, say, 4 years' time, that £100 is worth much less because of inflation. The company gains, the taxman loses. And the company has had use of the money, interest free.

The figure included under deferred taxation is therefore important because:

■ It shows the extent of one type of government subsidy to the company.

■ Although called deferred tax, it will probably never be paid and if paid will cost the company much less.

■ It is an important source of long-term finance to companies.

### Deferred payments:

Sometimes when a company buys another company, the money or shares are to be paid in future years. This has several advantages for the purchasing company:

■ It avoids dilution of the equity. For example: suppose Company A buys Company B paying in A's shares. B is making £100 profit. If half these shares are paid in two years' time, there will be more profits for the existing shareholders of A than there would be if all the shares were issued now. Because the earnings per share are greater now, the share price could go up. When the remaining shares have to be paid, the profits may be higher, so the earnings per share will not fall.

■ If it is cash that is being paid, the deferred payment will help reduce Company A's bank overdraft. When the payment becomes due the acquired Company B might have earned enough profits to pay the next instalment. So that B's own profits help it to pay the company.

Look for deferred payments, they may be one way of hiding the company's shortage of cash, and liquid resources.

Sometimes the company may owe money for acquisitions which will not appear in the Balance Sheet. Any such debts will appear in the Notes as **contingent liabilities.**

'Contingent' just means that the extent of the liability depends on something happening. For example, the exact payment may be determined by the level of profits achieved. Such deals are attractive to the seller because they give him the opportunity to get more for his business. The buyer likes them because he gets profits now but pays later. And he pays with the profits made by the company he bought.

The worker should look for any contingent liabilities and see how important they are in relation to the total profits and assets of the company, because:

▪ When the management has any such specific motivation to maximize profits, the worker may suffer.

▪ The company must go on increasing its profits to pay the contingent liabilities or deferred payments. A fall in profits may put the company under considerable financial strain, bringing redundancies and sackings.

▪ It is an advantage for a company to owe money which does not appear in the Balance Sheet. The company's apparent financial strength will make it far easier to do business. It may help the share price to go higher.

### Loans:

Sometimes a company may show its loans as a deferred liability, instead of as a source of capital, in the Capital Employed side of the Balance Sheet. This is the effect on the Balance Sheet:

**Balance Sheet A:**

| Assets | £2000 | Financed by ordinary shares: £500 |
| | | Long-term loans: £1500 |
| | £2000 | £2000 |

**Balance Sheet B:**

| Assets | £2000 | Financed by ordinary shares: £500 |
| Less deferred liabilities of | £1000 | Loans: £500 |
| | £1000 | £1000 |

These simple Balance Sheets are for the same company, but in B the directors have treated part of the long-term loans as a deferred liability. A casual look at Balance Sheet B might suggest that the company was much less highly-geared (see pages 128–29) than in Balance Sheet A.

### Pensions:

In the Balance Sheet shown on page 118 there is a deferred liability of £4,077,000 for pension rights. Pensions are discussed in greater detail on pages 57–60. When a company shows a deferred liability of pension payments this is what has happened: the company has guaranteed the workers certain pension rights, but instead of paying the money into a fund the company has kept the money in the business to finance expansion, choosing to build up pension debts rather than an independent fund.

# Employment of Capital: the assets side of the Balance Sheet:

The three main parts in this side of the Balance Sheet are:

■ **Fixed assets:** assets the company owns and does not intend reselling (factories, machines).

■ **Current assets:** assets that are or are expected to be cash within a year.

■ **Current liabilities:** money owed that is expected to be paid within a year.

There may also be reference to **goodwill.**

### Fixed assets:

The main fixed assets are: **land, buildings, machinery (for plant and office equipment).** Companies are required to distinguish between land and building and plant and machinery, and to indicate how they are valued and any changes in them during the year. Normally the company will print a table in the Note to the Accounts showing this information.

### Freehold property:

**Look for the valuation of freehold property.** There is no obligation on the company to revalue properties, and when the value is included at cost there is no obligation to give the date on which the property was bought. Sometimes the company's bank overdraft can be a clue to the real value of the company's property: look to see if the overdraft is 'secured' – i.e. a mortgage. It may be secured for more than the book value of the company's property.

▧ The 1972 Accounts of Francis Parker, showed land of £2.4 million but a bank overdraft of £6.7 million.

**Freehold property can often be a source of hidden wealth in a company.**

▧ In 1971 the Lloyds Bank Report and Accounts showed £111.5 million of property. In 1972 it was announced that this was worth an extra £160 million: three times Lloyds' annual wage bill.

**Look for the amount of freehold property.**

The existence of valuable freehold property gives the firm greater financial stability: the company can borrow money from the bank using the property as security and so survive difficult trading conditions more easily.

▧ Alfred Herbert (a machine tool manufacturer) had accumulated losses in the years 1970–72 of £8 million; the number of people who have lost their jobs would have been much greater if the company had not owned its large works in Coventry.

**Resist management attempts to sell freehold property, even though they make assurances that the business will be continued.**

A valuable property content may make the company vulnerable to a takeover, with the sale of the property and consequent loss of jobs:

▧ In the 1969 Report and Accounts of Gamages, property was shown to be valued at £1,987,000. In September 1970 Sterling Guarantee Trust bid £3.5 million for the whole of the company. By October they succeeded in their bid and paid £5.75 million. In December 1970 they formed a joint development company valuing Gamages' Holborn site alone at £6.25 million. The Gamages shop in Holborn has been demolished to make way for offices.

**Look to see if the freehold property has been depreciated** (see page 161). Where a company depreciates its freehold property it is saying that the property is worth less this year than it was last. This practice can substantially understate the real value of the assets: Barclays Bank pretax profits were reduced by £5.6 million in 1972 because of their depreciation of freehold and long leasehold property.

**Leasehold property:**

Leasehold property is property that the company doesn't own, but occupies for a fixed rent, that will be increased at a specified time in the future. (In recent years there has been a tendency for such rents to be reviewed at least every seven years.) Leasehold property differs from rented property in that the tenant has security of tenure and stability of rent for the length of the lease, whereas in rented property the tenant would probably be on a month or three months' notice.

At each review the rent on leasehold property is raised, generally to the current market rate. As rents have been rising quickly over the last ten years or so, this often means that companies are occupying leasehold very cheaply. The results of this are:

■ The leasehold property may be much more valuable than it appears in the Report and Accounts. This is particularly so because of amortization (which is similar to depreciation). The company assumes that the lease will be worth nothing at the end of its life, and therefore writes off part of the value of the lease each year. But if rents are rising the tenant could re-let the building at a higher rent than he is paying, and the value of the lease would therefore be higher than its written down value in the Balance Sheet.

■ The rent review may mean a sudden massive increase in overheads. To maintain his profits the businessman will try to respond by reducing his wage bill (sacking workers), increasing productivity or putting up his prices.

**Plant, machinery and motor vehicles:**

In a Note to the Accounts there will be a record of the value of plant and machinery, with the amount of depreciation written off in the year. The total depreciation figure for any year (which may include amortization of leasehold properties and depreciation of freehold properties) will be equal to the depreciation figure appearing in the Profit and Loss Account.

Be cautious: plant and machinery may be worth much less than the value in the Balance Sheet. Technological development may make the machines completely unsaleable and therefore worth only scrap value. But sometimes these non-property assets may be worth more than, or at least as much as, the depreciated value in the Balance Sheet. This can happen to:

■ An industry with little technological development.

> ■ There has been no substantial technological change in large parts of the wool textile industry over the last 50 years. Some mills are still using machinery that was in use before World War II. This will have been depreciated to almost nothing in the company's Balance Sheet but is still saleable, especially when wool products are in demand.

■ A company owning ships. Ships are valued in a similar way to property. The price or value of a ship is determined by its ability to provide an income, by being chartered at the going market rate. As many ships have a very long life, ships frequently increase in value, although they are depreciated in the Report and Accounts.

> ■ In September 1972 the Sheaf Steam Shipping Company sold one of its ships – Sheafmount – for £1.8 million. In the accounts it was valued at £900,000.

### Research and Development:

Some companies show research and development as a fixed asset. This is important.

Research and development money has been spent on research projects developing new products. Some companies argue that money spent in this way is almost the same as money spent on plant and equipment: instead of buying assets that produce profits, the company is buying a stock of knowledge that produces profits.

The research and development expenditure is not an asset like a piece of property. It has little value to the bank; it is not an asset that can be used as security to borrow money.

Turning research and development money into an asset is called **capitalizing the expenditure.** The alternative is to write the expenditure off against revenue: that means it is treated as a normal business expense that has to be charged before arriving at the profit figure.

If research and development expenditure is capitalized and is not deducted as a cost of production, profits appear higher than they would otherwise; but the quality of the company's assets is reduced. If research and development is written off against revenue, profits are depressed but the assets are of a much higher quality. Often companies will capitalize research and development, or similar expenses, to inflate profits artificially.

■ The Rolls Royce 1968 Balance Sheet shows capitalized research and development of £12 million. In 1969 the company spent a further £14,418,000, of which £4,132,000 was turned into a research and development asset.

■ The Brook Street Bureau used to capitalize the development costs of opening a new employment branch.

### Investments:
Some companies show their investments as fixed assets. Investments are simply shares in other companies. Sometimes there is a distinction between trade investments and other investments.

**Trade investments** are generally investments that have been bought to be held for ever in companies in a similar business. Other investments are generally shares that have been bought because the company hopes to make money on them in a short period of time. It is becoming increasingly common for manufacturing companies to have investments quite unconnected with their business.

■ Nottingham Manufacturing, the knitwear company, has investments of over £8 million. Its annual profits are slightly under £8 million.

■ Rubery Owen, the private engineering company, with 13,000 employees, has investments of over £2 million.

Often these shares have been bought with the retained profits of the company. Companies buy shares with their profits rather than spend money on new equipment which could provide jobs because:
■ Investments are **more liquid.** This means that they can be sold easily and are equivalent to cash. This increases the financial strength of the company – quoted investments are as good as cash, whereas plant and equipment is rarely instantly resaleable.

■ They give a **more secure** income – dividend income may not give such a good return as money invested in plant and machinery, but it is more stable than trading profits because companies rarely pay all their profits out in dividends and so can maintain the same level of dividends even when profits fall. It is also much less trouble to look after a collection of shares than to run a factory.

■ Investments have fewer risks. Although the price of shares on the Stock Market may fall, they do not carry the same risks and obligations as a labour force.

■ Because investment income itself has these attractions, companies with a high percentage of investment income are generally more highly rated on the Stock Market: i.e. their share prices are higher.

For the worker the trend is important: it gives companies greater financial strength independently of their productive activities. By reducing the importance of the manufacturing operation it may encourage management to resist any demands from the workers for longer than they might otherwise do.

**Remember:**

Frequently the shares are bought with retained profits. This is the surplus taken from the workers after the taxman and shareholders have been paid. The product of the workers' effort could be helping the company strengthen itself against the workers themselves.

**Goodwill:**

Goodwill is a **non-tangible asset** – it is not an asset you can touch in the same way you can touch plant and machinery. There are two main types of goodwill:

■ Goodwill arising on **consolidation.** When a company buys another company it often pays above that company's asset value. The extra amount is called goodwill – the value of the business name, trading connexions and so on.

Goodwill that arises in this way may not always be worth as much as it says. Companies are often over-valued in takeovers. This happens because the bidder is so anxious to get the biddee's agreement that it is willing to over-pay.

If the deal is being paid for with shares, it is easier to overpay because the bidder's shares may be so highly valued by the Stock Market that the acquisition still seems relatively cheap to the bidder.

■ A more important goodwill item is one that frequently does not appear in the accounts:

### The trade mark

Many companies have trade marks and trading names that are in themselves extremely valuable – Coca Cola, Marks & Spencers for example. Frequently no mention is made of this value in the accounts and these two companies in fact put no value on the goodwill of their name; although, in the event of the company being sold, they would raise a substantial amount of money. Even if there is no intention to sell the company, banks will generally be happier to lend money to a company with a well-known name than to a company that is completely unknown.

**Other non-tangible assets, such as a monopoly position, or a dramatic change in the trading background, can make the Balance Sheet an unreliable guide to the company's wealth.**

### Current assets:
The main categories are:

### Stocks:
Stocks are **the goods the company has bought** and **goods the company has made but not delivered.**

A Note to the Accounts will say that stocks have been valued at the lower of cost or net realizable value (sale price). This cannot be relied upon. Clearly many goods can lose their value entirely: dresses go out of fashion; machinery becomes outdated. In 1971 Alfred Herbert reduced the value of its stocks by over £1 million because its machines were thought to be obsolete.

Similarly stocks may be worth much more than the valuation in the accounts. This applies particularly to land held for development. But in a period of rapid inflation, the value of raw materials and even finished goods can rise substantially:

■ In Tate & Lyle's 1972 Accounts, the stock figure included 250,000 tons of sugar valued at £24 a ton. The market price at that time was nearer £200 a ton.

The valuation of stocks can be an important way in which profits are hidden (see pages 154–57). But in the case of public companies the price of the shares is determined by the level of profits and businessmen are judged by their ability to produce profits, so public companies do not usually hide their profits by undervaluing the stock.

There are two exceptions:

■ When a company has only recently become a public company, and

■ When there has been an exceptionally profitable year and the company wants to keep a reserve of profit.

Companies rarely admit that their stocks are worth less than they paid for them, even though this may often be the case. This is because:

■ Trading conditions may change and goods that are unmarketable (and therefore worth less than the company paid for them) may become more marketable.

■ It may seem an admission of failure to admit that stocks are worth less than was paid for them. Businessmen don't want to admit failure.

■ If the stocks are worth less, it means the shareholders lose money either in profits or in the value of the company's assets.

There is no certain way of telling from the Balance Sheet how correctly stocks are valued or how much hidden profit there is in the stock figures. However, something can be learnt from the stock figure.

If stocks are much higher than in the previous year and there has not been a big increase in prices generally, it could mean several things:

■ The company can't sell what it is making.

■ The company has bought in a lot of materials, expecting an increase in demand for its products, or expecting a sharp increase in the price of raw materials.

■ The company may be deferring profit. It may be hoarding goods ready for delivery, so that the profit on them comes in the next year's accounts.

Workers should use their own knowledge of what is lying around factories and warehouses to decide if any of these apply.

The speed with which the stocks are turned round every year is some indication of the management's control of what is happening in the company. The annual **stock turn** is worked out simply by dividing the value of total sales by the value of stocks.

**For example:** If sales are £20 million and stocks are £5 million, the stock turn is 4. This means that very roughly, it takes three months for something the company buys to go through the business and be sold as a finished good. Clearly the stock turn varies from industry to industry: in the retail trade, especially supermarket chains, the stock is sold quickly so the stock turn is very high. In 1973 Tesco's stock turn was 11.6. In manufacturing industries it is much less, though many companies seem to aim for an entirely arbitrary stock turn of four times a year.

To some extent workers will be able to judge from their own knowledge of the company how fast stocks are being turned over.

### Debtors:

The debtors figure represents money owed to the company for products it has sold. Sometimes there may be bad debts – money which the directors think will never be paid. Companies are often very slow in deciding a debt is bad, but if a customer goes bankrupt, money owed is generally recognized as a bad debt immediately. Making allowance for bad debts will reduce profits.

### Cash:

This is cash in the bank. Any investments or loans that appear as current assets are generally as good as cash and are expected to be turned into cash within a year.

### Current liabilities:

### Creditors:

This is money owed by the company to their suppliers. Because it is money that the company is using, it is helping to finance the business. But it is expected to be paid within a year – otherwise it would appear as a long-term source of funds. Companies in financial difficulties will often try and pay their suppliers (creditors) later than normal.

You can tell how long it takes a company to pay its bills.

■ The following sum will show how many weeks' credit the company is using:

$$52 \div \frac{\text{sales}}{\text{creditors}}$$

Suppose a company's annual sales are £5 million and creditors are shown at £600,000. The sum would be

$$52 \div \frac{\text{£5 million}}{\text{£0.6 million}}$$

$$= 52 \div 8.33$$

$$= 6.24$$

On average, the company pays its bills after six weeks.

Compare this with the figure for earlier years.

Compare the creditors figure with the debtors (money owed to the company) figure: does the company owe more than it is owed?

The average payment period varies substantially from industry to industry. Big retailing companies like Tesco give no credit but use the credit of their suppliers to finance their business.

### Tax:

This is money owed to the taxman. The taxman is a valuable source of short-term finance for business. The Inland Revenue tax year runs from 1 April to 31 March, but many companies' tax years have different ending dates. Tax is payable 9 months after the end of the taxman's year in which the company's accounting year ends.

For example, a company with its year ending on 31 December 1975 will be assessed for tax on the profits earned in that year but will not have to pay the tax until 1 January 1977.

### Short-term borrowings and bank overdrafts:

This is money that the company owes to the bank and other money that has to be repaid in a year. Often this is extremely misleading.

In theory, bank overdrafts are provided on seven days' notice – the bank can demand the repayment of that money within that time. In fact, the money might be used to finance stocks which often can't be sold immediately and in some cases may finance machinery and equipment.

> ■ In the 1972 Accounts of the Savoy Hotel Company, £2.5 million of bank advances were shown as long-term capital, even though the overdraft was subject to annual review.

The bank overdraft of a company often remains materially unchanged from year to year or, even if it is changed, doesn't drop below some fixed level. In such a case the bank overdraft is probably being used as long-term finance for a company. Companies will continue to do this, rather than raise long-term money because:

■ The interest rate on bank overdrafts varies. The interest rate on a long-term loan remains stable and therefore the company cannot benefit from any fall in interest rates.

■ A company's demand for credit may fluctuate during the year. With a bank overdraft it is only charged for the money it uses. But with long-term finance it is paying interest on the same amount of money throughout the year.

■ Although the company may use bank money as long-term finance, it is not called this in the Balance Sheet. In assessing the company's credit-worthiness or the value of the company's shares investors and suppliers may concentrate on long-term indebtedness: if the company is heavily committed with long-term debt, the security of the ordinary shareholder's money is reduced. By using bank borrowing, the company may be able to disguise its total long-term borrowings.

There are disadvantages to using bank overdrafts as long-term money. These have important implications for the workers: the bank may start asking for its money back. In recent years, as banks have tried to maximize their profits much more aggressively, this has started to happen. The company will then have to take action to find the money – cut back on stocks, on the level of activity (i.e. manufacturing hours), and debtors.

*Look for:* **the size of bank overdrafts and their consistency over the years in relation to the current assets of the company. The larger the overdraft as a percentage of total current assets, the greater the vulnerability to the bank's intervention.**

> ■ In 1971 the Midland Bank was instrumental in appointing a new Chairman to the Board of the Belfast Ropeworks company. The Company was making losses of over £600,000 annually. In the following shake-up there were substantial redundancies.

### Dividends:

This is money that the company has committed itself to paying out in dividends during the year; but which is not actually paid until after the year has ended. It is not an addition to the dividends declared that appear in the Profit and Loss Account.

# 12.

# Limited liability

This chapter explains the advantages and disadvantages of different forms of company and their implications for workers. It starts with partnerships which are relatively informal, then describes limited liability companies followed by the differences between public and private companies.

## Partnerships:

This is the form of 'company' chosen by many small businesses. A partnership is a loosely organized structure for a business: it is just a collection of people who are jointly carrying on the same business, with a view to making a profit. Anyone who shares in the profits of the business is considered a partner and all the partners are liable for the debts and liabilities of the partnership.

These are the advantages of a partnership:

■ It is a very flexible organization. The members of a partnership may have an agreement among themselves about the distribution of profit and the way in which the business is run. But a partnership does not have to register itself as a company and therefore its operation is not governed by any formal rules.

■ Because the members of the partnership are personally liable for the debts of the business, the accounts are not open to public inspection. A partnership's profits are therefore completely secret.

■ There are tax advantages: partners of a firm are treated as self-employed people and thus have a wide range of expenses they can legitimately claim against their tax bill.

These are the **disadvantages of running a business as a partnership**:

■ Membership of a partnership is limited to twenty people. Any business carried on for profit that involves the association of more than twenty people must be registered as a company.

This limit does not apply to solicitors, accountants or members of the Stock Exchange. The result of this is that several large and profitable organizations keep their profits completely secret. Although solicitors are forbidden by law from becoming companies, stockbrokers and accountants are not and some have done so.

It is possible to have a *limited partnership*. In such a firm the limited partners are liable only for the capital or property they contribute, with the other 'general' partners being liable for all the debts of the firm. But the limited partner cannot participate in the management of the firm, otherwise he loses his limited liability. It is this separation of management from capital that has made limited partnerships relatively unattractive, although a few do exist.

This restriction on the size of a partnership means that expansion can be difficult: the only way in which a partnership can expand is to bring in new partners with new capital. With more members the partnership may become unwieldy and might quickly reach the ceiling level of twenty members. In addition, the larger the sums of money that are committed the greater the risk involved in unlimited liability.

■ It is difficult for people to leave partnerships. If a partner wants to leave – or dies – his share can only be realized by liquidating the funds of the business: there are no shares that can be sold. In other words, it is difficult for the business to exist as something separate from the wealth of the people who own it.

**What this means to the workers:**

■ It is difficult to find information about the profits of partnerships.

■ The security of the business is only as great as the interest or lives of the partners.

# Companies:

There are three forms of companies:

1. Limited Liability Companies
2. Unlimited Liability Companies
3. Companies Limited by Guarantee

## Limited Liability Companies:

All but a minute proportion of the $1\frac{1}{4}$ million companies registered in the UK are **limited liability companies**. Limited liability can be summarized as follows: the ownership of the company's wealth and the right to its profits rests in the hands of the owners of the company's shares. These shares represent (often very tenuously) the original money that was put up to start the company. The shareholders' liability (financial obligation) is limited to that money. This means that the company can borrow money from the bank, buy as many supplies as it likes, and the shareholders have no obligation to meet any debts that might arise. If a company goes bankrupt – cannot pay its debts – the shareholders have no obligation to pay those debts.

> When Rolls-Royce went bankrupt in 1971, its debts were estimated to amount to £61 million. The shareholders, who had received dividends over the years, didn't have to meet any of these debts. It was the company's suppliers who faced the prospect of footing the bill.
> In the event, generous cash gifts from the government meant that the creditors were paid and the shareholders also got 50p a share, instead of nothing.

**In other words limited liability offers a company all the advantages that partnerships do not have:**
- **Ease of raising capital for expansion.**
- **Liability of the capitalist (provider of the capital) is limited.**
- **Continuity of the business; ownership of the company can be transferred by the sale of shares.**

The great advantage of limited liability to the capitalist is that risk is limited although he has the prospect of unlimited reward.

> In 1930, Office Cleaning Services Ltd was formed by the Goodcliffe family, with £200. That is the total money they have had at risk and the family, which still owns the company, now making profits of £2 million, is probably worth at least £8 million.
> In 1964 Ray Turner started the SOS Employment Bureau with £20,000. In 1973 he sold out for £1.75 million.

The result of this is that many of the risks of running a business are borne by the company's creditors – those companies which sell products to the company and are therefore owed money. To protect the interests of other business enterprises, therefore, the government requires companies to produce an annual Report and Accounts. If limited liability was not accompanied by some disclosure of information about the company, it would be possible for other businesses to lose substantial sums of money from directors diverting a company's money into the hands of its shareholders.

### Public and private limited liability companies:

There are two types of limited liability company, private and public.

Many people are confused by the word **public.** It has nothing to do with nationalized industries – which are often referred to as the **public sector.** A **public company** is a company in which the public can hold shares. A **private company** is a company where there is some restriction on the buying and selling of shares. Both public and private companies are part of what is often called the **private sector** of the economy. Most public companies have their shares quoted on the Stock Exchange and are therefore referred to as **quoted companies.**

In detail, the main features of **private companies are:**

■ A restriction on the right to transfer shares. Generally, shareholders can sell their shares only with the permission of the Board of Directors.

■ A limitation on the number of shareholders to fifty (excluding employees or ex-employers).

■ A prohibition on asking the public to buy shares in the company.

A **public company** is one where the directors cannot restrict the purchase and sale of shares, where the shares can be offered to the public and where there is no restriction on the number of shareholders.

As a result, all but a small number of public companies have their shares quoted on the Stock Exchange.

**Why do capitalists choose a public rather than a private company?**

When a businessman turns his private company into a public company, he suffers **two disadvantages:**

■ Loss of complete control over his company. Even if he

controls a majority of the shares, the minority shareholders want to see profits every year. This closes a whole range of tax avoidance techniques which have the effect of reducing profits. The company now has an obligation to produce profits every year – it cannot sacrifice profits and dividends one year so as to finance expansion.

■ Less secrecy. The Stock Exchange has more stringent requirements on the disclosure of information than the government. Also, public companies are open to scrutiny by the financial press, which tends to criticize companies that don't provide detailed information.

Directors are willing to put up with these difficulties because there are advantages:

■ Taxation. Public companies' shares are more easily sold than private companies'. In this way, rich men can overcome some of the problems of death duties. Also directors can receive their income from selling shares that rise in value (and are taxed at 30 per cent) rather than in high salaries (which can be taxed at up to three times as much).

■ Raising capital. A company can raise long-term capital to finance its business by selling shares to the public. Although now less than 10 per cent of industry's new capital is raised in this way (most comes from retained profits and the banks) this was once an important source of capital and was the main reason for companies going public.

■ Expansion. Becoming a public company gives directors a new currency: the company's shares. These can be issued to buy other companies, and this expansion need not be restricted to traditional business of the original company.

> ■ In 1971 the Ray Turner Group – owners of the SOS Employment Bureau – raised £740,000 from the sale of its shares to the public. The prospectus said it would be used to finance expansion of the employment bureau. Later in 1971 some of this was spent buying a publishing company.

> ■ In March 1973 a company called Levex raised £556,000 by selling its shares to the public. Its prospectus said that the money would be used to expand the company's double-knit-jersey business. In August the company spent £550,000 buying a fabric wholesaling business.

■ In 1963 a small dress company called Raybeck sold its shares to the public. Ten years later, after the issue of numerous shares in acquisitions, over 50 per cent of the company's profits came from retailing clothes.

## The implications for workers:

If you work for a public company, check how long it has been a public company. If it has become public only recently (or if the private company that you work for is going public) check the following:

■ Did the directors sell any shares?
■ Did the company itself raise any new money?
■ What did the directors say about the future?

(Page 36 tells you how to get hold of the prospectus offering the shares for sale.)

### Because:

■ Some companies go public just before things start going wrong so the directors get the most they can for their shares.
■ Some companies go public because the directors want to expand in other types of business.
■ Some companies go public because the directors want to pull out or direct their personal wealth elsewhere.

## Unlimited liability companies:

These companies are incorporated as companies rather than partnerships, to avoid the restriction on the number of members a partnership can have. The directors and shareholders are all personally liable for the debts of the company. As this is a massive liability if the company is large, unlimited liability companies are unusual. One important exception is C & A – the department store. This company is unlimited so that it can benefit from the secrecy that comes with unlimited liability: no annual accounts showing the annual profit have to be published.

## Companies limited by guarantee:

These are companies without any share capital. This means profits cannot be distributed, as there are no shareholders. For that reason no capitalist will form a company limited by guarantee. Sunderlandia – a building company owned and controlled by the workers – is a company limited by guarantee.

# 13.

# The concealment of profits

There are many ways in which the Profit and Loss Account can hide the true profitability of a company. They are used by both public and private companies.

## Valuation of stock:

Three ways in which the valuation of stocks can be used to hide profits:

■ Undervaluing the stocks at the end of the year.

■ Including all overheads in the valuation of stocks.

■ Employing a system of valuation known as 'last in – first out'. (This is not allowed in the UK but it is common in the USA.)

### Undervaluing stocks:

Here is a simple demonstration of how a company arrives at its gross trading profit, i.e. the profit before charging any of the running expenses of the business:

The company's gross profit is sales minus cost of raw materials and stock sold. It then deducts all other expenses – labour and other overheads. The scope for manipulation is in the calculation of the cost of stock sold.

**How to adjust profits through manipulation of stock values**

| | A | B |
|---|---|---|
| 1. Stock at the beginning of the year | 100 | 100 |
| 2. Stock bought during the year | 1000 | 1000 |
| 3. Total stock | 1100 | 1100 |
| 4. Value of stock at the end of the year | 100 | — |
| 5. Cost of stock sold | 1000 | 1100 |
| 6. Sale price of stock | 2000 | 2000 |
| 7. Therefore gross trading profit (before expenses and overheads) (6 minus 5) | 1000 | 900 |

If the company undervalues its stock at the end of the year (line 4) the gross trading profit will be reduced. Suppose the company had said the stock was worthless (column B) then the cost of stock sold would be 1100 (line 5) and the gross trading profits (line 7) would be 900.

In this way the company can hide some of its profit in any one year and can bring it back into the Profit and Loss Account by slightly altering stock valuations in future years. If the stock is undervalued, all the surplus comes through to the company's gross trading profit when it is sold. The profit can be continually deferred by writing down (undervaluing) the stock at the end of each year.

The company's accountants will co-operate with a company employing this technique to understate profits. It is good accounting practice to take the most cautious view in drawing up accounts. The accountants will be willing to assume the businessman knows better than they the value of the stock. They are, after all, employed and paid by the directors, so it is not wise to disagree with them too strongly. This particular technique of reducing profits is widely used by private companies. Public companies may use the technique in two circumstances:

■ **When a company has only recently become a public company.**

As a private company the company will have been trying to understate profits to reduce payments to the taxman. As a public company the shareholders will want to see high profits. In this case the company may start drawing on its reserve of stock profits. The same applies to a private company that is taken over by a public company.

■ **In a very good year.**

If a company has an exceptionally profitable year, the directors may feel that the shareholders will be satisfied with a lower profit figure than has actually been achieved. In this case attempts will be made to keep some of the profit over for the next year when trading conditions may be a bit more difficult. This became more widely practised when profit controls were introduced as companies can be penalized for making high profits.

### Overheads included in valuation:

In the diagram on page 155 the cost of goods sold was increased by saying some stocks were worthless. Costs can also be increased by including a lot of overheads.

It costs more to produce a product than the cost of raw materials. By the time raw materials become finished goods, various costs have been incurred: **variable costs** (those that are connected directly to the manufacturing of the product) – fuel bills and some wages, for instance; and **fixed costs** (the overheads incurred in the business regardless of the level of activity) – rents, rates and some wages. The company has to decide which of these costs are included in the valuation of the stock. Some companies include all overheads; some companies exclude all overheads.

■ *Suppose a company has spent £1 million on advertising a product during the year. If the company includes all this as a cost in one year, (line 5 on page 55) it thereby increases the cost of the stock that has been sold, and reduces profits.*

**The more overheads that are included as a cost of stock, the lower profits will be.**

The effect of these differing accounting techniques is on the timing of profits. A company which writes off all its overheads in one year will have higher profits in future years. A company that increases profits in one year by deferring the cost of its overheads will have lower profits in future years because it will still be bearing the cost of those overheads.

It is important for the worker to know how the company treats its overheads because it is a guide to future profitability. A company which reduces profits by writing off all overheads in one year is obviously capable of big profits in future years.

**The 'last in – first out' method:**

This is a method of stock valuation used in America but not allowed in this country. It is a way of eliminating stock profits from a company's Profit and Loss Accounts.

*Suppose a company has stocks at the beginning of the year of 100 tons of steel. During the year the company buys and sells more steel so that at the end of the year, it still has 100 tons of steel as stock. Under the 'last in, first out' method all the stock used during the year will be assumed to have cost the price of the last consignment bought.*

In arriving at the profit figure all stock is assumed to have cost the most recent (usually the highest) of the year and profits are thus reduced.

> ■ A note in English Calico's 1973 Accounts says: 'Stocks are valued at the lower of cost or net realizable value . . . For the American Thread Company, cost is determined partly on the "last in, first out" method which is substantially lower than replacement value.'

**In other words, the stocks are valued at less than they are worth.**

Companies are obliged to say on what basis stocks are valued; often this is limited to saying 'at the lower of cost or realizable value'. Some public companies give more details about the inclusion of overheads.

# Treatment of Research and Development (R&D):

Profits can be reduced by treating all Research and Development as an expense of the business as it arises. Profits can be increased by treating the spending as either a capital cost and writing it off over a period of years or as a capital asset.

Many companies spend money researching and developing new products. This money is spent before the products produce any profit. Some companies argue that it distorts profits to treat this as an expense of the business. In such a case the Research and Development expenditure will appear in the Balance Sheet and be written off over the years in which the product is making a contribution to profits.

Look in the Balance Sheet for items such as 'deferred R & D expenditure'.

&#9632; In the last Balance Sheet before it went bankrupt, Rolls-Royce had an item of £4.13 million credited to its balance sheet as an R & D asset.

&#9632; British and Commonwealth Shipping has been developing a new machine tool since 1967. All its costs were written off profits in each year, although it has made no contribution to profits.

It is hard to know when companies are writing off development cost against current profits because there is no obligation on them to say whether they are doing so and no obligation to itemize total research costs.

Many public companies do so; look and see if they do in the statement of accounting policies.

**Workers need to do some guessing here. Is the company involved in an industry for which research and development is important? Does the firm have a Research and Development Department? If it does, and there is no item for Research and Development in the Balance Sheet, then the cost is being written off current profits, and management claims that profits are low are misleading. Profits appear low because management is spending money developing the next money-making product.**

Most property companies employ a similar technique to boost profits, it is often called a **Capital Development Reserve**. It works like this: It takes time to buy and build property. During this time the company spends money but receives no rent. As a result it is losing money. To prevent a loss appearing in the Profit and Loss Account the company defers the cost of the development or assumes a rental income during its development. The result is the same. Profits are boosted by including a transfer from reserves in the Balance Sheet.

# Depreciation:

The meaning of depreciation is explained on page 48. There are three ways in which the depreciation charge can be used to depress profits.

These are:

■ The system employed.
■ The rate charged.
■ What is depreciated.

### System employed:

There are two systems that can be employed: 'straight line' or 'reducing balance'. The reducing balance method of depreciation will reduce profits in the early years of a machine's life.

*Assume a machine costs £1,200 and is expected to last 10 years.*

*The company can EITHER: assume the scrap value of the machine at the end of the 10-year period will be (say) £130, which means that £1,070 (£1,200 minus £130) has to be written off the value of the machine over the 10 years that it is in use, i.e. £107 a year. This the* straight line *method.*

**or**

*A company can assume a machine will fall in value by a fixed percentage each year, say 20 per cent, until the last year of its life, also giving it a scrap value of £130. This is the reducing balance method.*

The **table below shows the difference between the two systems.**

The effect on profits of different systems of depreciation:

| | Reducing Balance | Straight Line |
|---|---|---|
| Cost of machine | £1200 | £1200 |
| Year 1 depreciation | 240 (20% of £1200) | 107 |
| Leaving residual value | 960 | 1093 |
| Year 2 depreciation | 192 (20% of £960) | 107 |
| Leaving residual value | 768 | 986 |
| Year 3 depreciation | 154 (20% of £768): | 107 |
| Residual value | 614 | 879 |
| Year 4 depreciation | 123 (20% of £614): | 107 |
| Residual value | 491 | 772 |
| Year 5 depreciation | 98 (20% of £491): | 107 |
| Residual value | 393 | 665 |
| Year 6 depreciation | 78 (20% of £393): | 107 |
| Residual value | 314 | 558 |
| Year 7 depreciation | 63 (20% of £314): | 107 |
| Residual value | 251 | 451 |
| Year 8 depreciation | 50 (20% of £251): | 107 |
| Residual value | 201 | 344 |
| Year 9 depreciation | 40 (20% of £201): | 107 |
| Residual value | 161 | 237 |
| Year 10 depreciation | 32 (20% of £161): | 107 |
| Residual value | 129 | 130 |

In the first four years the charge under the reducing balance method is greater and so profits will be lower.

The method of depreciation used will probably be referred to in one of the Notes to the Accounts, or in the note showing the accounting policies used.

### The rate charged:

A company has to decide how long its machine will last, and how much it will be worth at the end of its life.

In the diagram above, if the directors decided that the machine would last only five years, the depreciation charge would double and profits would be lower. Companies sometimes state the rate of depreciation they are charging, but rarely give the life expectancy of the machines.

It is hard to know if directors are being conservative in their estimates. Use your own knowledge of the industry to help you make a decision. Read the notes on the depreciation policies. These may give the percentage charged where the reducing balance system is used. The higher the rate of depreciation, the lower the profits.

Some companies have introduced a new **inflation factor** into their depreciation policy, increasing the depreciation charge further and thus depressing profits (see pages 105–109). This depreciation is not recognized by the taxman, so it is shown separately and will probably be referred to in the Balance Sheet as a 'depreciation reserve'.

> ■ In 1971 Guest Keen and Nettlefold's profits were £3.7 million lower because of a special provision 'for the reduced purchasing power of money'. The accumulated reserve of this extra depreciation amounted to £23.4 million. In most companies that would have been shown as profit.

### What is depreciated:

Some companies increase their depreciation charge and reduce profits by writing off assets that rise in value, such as property and buildings. Some companies depreciate freehold property.

> ■ Barclays Bank 1972 profits were reduced by £5·6 million because of the depreciation of freehold property.

Although the depreciation of freehold property is unusual now, it was more common in the past before the boom of property prices. Some companies' freehold property is still valued after depreciation years ago, even though it is no longer depreciated.

Depreciation of buildings as opposed to land is much more common among industrial companies, although it is not always realistic to assume that offices and factories fall in value over the years.

Look at the Notes to the Balance Sheet. They will show whether land and buildings are being depreciated.

# Mistakes and exceptional items:

Businessmen make mistakes; products become obsolete, investments lose money. These losses can either be charged as a normal business expense like wages – and so reduce profits – or can be treated exceptionally – leaving pre-tax profits unaffected. If treated as exceptional – they may be written off 'below the line' (deducted from profits after tax), or the figure may be written off reserves.

The reserves item of the Balance Sheet was explained on pages 123–124.

However the exceptional items are treated, the result is the same in the end:

*Suppose a company has accumulated profits (i.e. reserves) in the Balance Sheet of £200. In a particular year it makes £100 pre-tax profit but also loses (after tax relief) £50 because one of its products becomes obsolete and has to be scrapped. There are three ways in which it could be treated.*

|  | 1 | 2 | 3 |
|---|---|---|---|
| Trading profit | 100 | 100 | 100 |
| Exceptional loss | 100 | — | — |
| Pretax profit | 000 | 100 | 100 |
| Tax | — | 50 | 50 |
|  | — | 50 | 50 |
| Exceptional | — | 50 | — |
| Transfer to Reserves | — | — | 50 |

*In Column 1 the company has written off the mistake against profits before arriving at the pre tax profit figure. It pays no tax on the £100 profits because the loss can be offset against any tax liabilities.*

*In Column 2 the company has written the exceptional item off after-tax profits. The loss is only £50 after tax because the full loss can be offset against the tax bill and so only costs the company half of the actual loss.*

*In Column 3 the loss will be written off Reserves in the Balance Sheet after the £50 profit has been added to them from the Profit and Loss Account. There will therefore be no net increase in the Reserves figure.*

*Although the first method may mean a fall in share prices, directors may feel this is desirable:*

■ *If they are newly appointed they can blame the loss on the past and when profits increase substantially the following year – when there are expected to be no exceptional items – they will get all the credit.*

■ *If the directors are controlling shareholders, knowing the real reason for the lack of profits they will not be unduly concerned about the fall but will be able to use the accounts when bargaining with the workers.*

■ *The directors are aware that the shareholders can put up with a bad year. They know they can blame other factors for the fall in profits and may use a loss to counter workers' demands for more money.*

The illustration is very extreme. In real life it may be a matter of £250,000 loss, compared to profits of £15 million.

A company's success in using exceptional items to depress apparent profits depends on secrecy; there will be no easy way of telling from the accounts that profits have been exceptionally depressed in this way.

But always look in the Notes to the Accounts to see if it says pre-tax profits have been arrived at after charging any exceptional items.

Exceptional items were itemized in the Wiggins Teape Accounts (page 103), but it was only after careful reading of the Notes that this became clear.

Directors usually choose the other ways of treating exceptional items (Columns 2 or 3) to hide incompetence. The pretax profit record is thus unaffected by exceptional items.

Many shareholders won't read the Notes to the Accounts, where there would be a record of the exceptional items. Profits on the **sale of property** can be treated in the same way. Adding these profits to Reserves helps to build up the assets of the company, without any distortion in the profit record.

Look closely at the Notes to the Accounts for reference to exceptional items, especially notes on the pre-tax profit figure and the changes in the Reserves. But this still cannot tell you whether the company is treating exceptional items as non-exceptional and not mentioning them in arriving at the pre-tax figure.

Exceptional items are important to workers because the Profit and Loss Account can be used to assess the potential profitability of the company. By the time the Profit and Loss Account is published, it is out of date. Workers are not negotiating over last year's profits, but over current and future years. The figure they are using as a basis should not be distorted by items that the management admits are exceptional and are unlikely to occur in the future.

# Warrant liabilities:

Some companies make products under guarantee. The terms of the guarantee have to be met, by giving services and parts free. It will cost the firm money. The firm can either make a provision for such liabilities when it sells its products (so reducing profits) or meet the costs as claims are satisfied.

Look to see whether such a provision exists – it will be shown as a deferred liability in the Balance Sheet, increasing each year as transfers are made from the Profit and Loss Account.

Treatment of this item has important implications for job security: Only by making provisions for such liabilities can directors and workers be sure that massive debts and therefore possible bankruptcy are not suddenly going to face a company.

> ■The Accounts of Herbert Ingersoll in 1971 said: 'No provision has been made in these accounts against any claims by customers for rectification work on machines supplied by the company.' In June 1972 the company was put into liquidation.

This and other conservative accounting techniques are important for the workers. A financially soundly-based company is less likely to go out of business.

But:

■ The businessman is interested in such sound financial structures because it reduces his reliance on the work force:

■ Conservatism in accounting techniques hides the wealth and profitability of the company. This hidden surplus is a justifiable target in bargaining.

# Taxes:

Pages 110–112 explain that although companies may show a 50 per cent tax charge in their Profit and Loss Account, they rarely pay this much.

Companies include a full tax charge in their accounts, but don't pay it. The surplus is kept in the **deferred taxation account**. Look in the Notes for:

■ The note on the composition of the tax figure. This will show the transfer to deferred taxation.

■ The increase in the deferred taxation or tax equalization figure: this is the amount of money that has been charged to the Profit and Loss Account but not actually paid.

# Treatment of income and sales:

Page 155 shows that the gross trading profit figure is arrived at by subtracting the cost of goods sold from the proceeds of their sale:

Sale price of goods: 2,000

Cost price of goods: 1,000

Gross trading profits: 1,000

Profits can be hidden by manipulation of the stock figure (pp. 154–6). They are also affected by the treatment of sales – if sales are brought forward profits are increased, if sales are deferred they are reduced.

Take a company that manufactures very large products – aeroplanes. If one of these was to be sold on the last day of the year, the company could defer the sale by one day, and reduce the sales figure and thus profits. The aeroplane would appear in the Balance Sheet at its cost – the profit element could not be included as a part of its value, as stocks are valued at the lower of cost or sale value.

A product is considered sold when the invoice is sent out, i.e. when the product is delivered. Companies cannot depress profits by not collecting their debts. They can depress profits temporarily by delivering slowly, though their freedom in this is restricted by commercial consideration: they may lose the orders if they are too slow. There is no sure way of telling if the company is deferring delivery of goods. Goods not delivered appear as stocks or work in progress in the Balance Sheet. If this figure is exceptionally large by comparison with earlier years and with the sales figure it may be because deliveries and sales are being deferred until the year has ended.

The deferring of sales is practised on a wider scale and more easily achieved in certain types of companies.

## Long-term contracts

Many construction and building companies are inolved in long-term contracts – bridge-building, road building etc. Shipbuilding companies also have long-term contracts. In many cases payment will not be made until the contract is completed. The businessman has to decide whether the profits on long-term contracts are credited to the Profit and Loss Account when the contract is completed or over the life of the contract.

If the profit is taken only on completion of the contract, profits will be deferred and thus hidden.

Although in many contracts **progress payments** are made, it is becoming rare to credit profits before the contract is completed. This means published profits fluctuate widely as the contracts are completed and there are long periods of low or no profits. It is easy to explain the practice from the businessman's point of view. In recent years there have been several dramatic examples of long-term contracts being less profitable than originally expected, because of unforeseen difficulties or inflation. At the same time there has been a growing concern among some investors about the quality of assets and profits rather than just their apparent size.

The more conservative the accounting techniques the better the quality of the company; it is a safer company with which to do business. It is both less likely to go bankrupt and more likely to survive any problems that do arise without serious disruption, such as paying its bills late and delivering goods late. A company that employs conservative accounting will generally provide greater security of employment for this reason.

Although conservative accounting is preferable from the workers' point of view, it is important to realize that it *is* conservative because:

■ The company is stronger than might at first appear.
■ There may be substantial reserves of profits, such as when long-term contracts are completed:

> ■ 'We believe that the £14.33 million profit is understated because this figure only relates to contracts completed in the year to 31/12/72 and the term completed is subject to all sorts of interpretations. The amount of profit held back in Work in Progress account has been estimated by a very well-informed source to be at least £25 million!' – Stockbrokers Sandleson, writing about Wimpeys, March 1974.

But some building companies are less conservative:

> ■ 'The group trading profit includes profits as contracts completed prior to 1st January 1973 and the results on current contracts based on valuations by officials of the company.' From accounts of French Kier Holdings.

A Note to the Accounts may refer to the way in which long-term contracts are treated, but in general it is very difficult to tell how far profits have been affected by differing accounting policies:

> ■ The profits of Crittall Hope were £4.2 million in 1972. In 1973 they fell to £1.1 million. During 1973 the company had been bought by its new owners Norcros, from Slater Walker Securities. *The Economist* commented on 10 August 1974:
>> 'Norcros takes a much more conservative view on the value of stocks, work-in-progress (particularly the taking of profits on uncompleted contracts) and possible debts than Mr Slater's management did. Unfortunately it is not possible to quantify how much this difference of valuation contributes to Crittall's loss. On today's accounting requirements there is no way in which the shareholder can find out how far Crittall's profits are affected by the perfectly legitimate, but widely differing, views that the new board takes on just how much its assets are worth.'

**Hire-Purchase sales:**

Under hire-purchase agreements the purchaser pays for the product he buys over a period of time. If he defaults in his payments the vendor can take back the product. The profits from the sale of goods under hire-purchase agreements can be credited either when the agreement is first signed or spread over the life of the agreement. If the second method is used profits will appear low and even lower if the profits are credited only when the final instalment is paid. A Note to the Accounts may disclose the way in which hire-purchase agreements are being treated. The same problem applies to goods provided in rental agreements, such as by car-hire firms.

■Curry's 1973 Accounts showed pre-tax profits of £6.9 million, but the company had £8.2 million worth of expected profit on unmatured hire-purchase agreements.

**Housebuilding:**

The profit on the sale of houses can be credited either:
■ When the customer places the deposit; or
■ When contracts are exchanged, i.e. shortly before occupation of the house.

The second will tend to defer and therefore reduce profits in any one year. Wimpeys are believed to credit profits on housebuilding only when the last house on the estate has been sold.

# Subsidiary and associate companies:

A subsidiary company is one in which the parent company holds over 50 per cent of the shares. An associate company is one in which another company holds over 20 per cent of the voting capital and exercises some control over the company's management.

The law requires that the profit of subsidiaries be **consolidated** i.e. included in the group profit figures. It is a recommendation of the Institute of Chartered Accountants that the share of an associate's profits be consolidated.

Some public companies do not consolidate the profits attributable to associates and thus hide the company's profitability.

> British and Commonwealth Shipping own 39 per cent of Safmarine, a South African Shipping Company. It does not consolidate these profits, so that the only contribution from Safmarine is the £640,000 worth of dividends, compared to British and Commonwealth's profits of £4.7 million. If B & C consolidated its holding, the contribution would be £2 million.

Failure to consolidate an associate company will reduce published profits, but there should be a Note in the Accounts drawing attention to this.

# 14.

# Investment grants

Investment grants were the predecessors of the system of capital allowances now current (see page 110). Investment grants were cash gifts to help pay for plant and machinery; capital allowances are tax rebates. The exact size of the grant varied, depending on the type of investment and location of the company. Investment grants still occur in the Profit and Loss Account because of these earlier commitments, and other cash grants are still made: **regional development grants** (for spending money in the development areas), **shipbuilding grants** (gifts to make British-built ships cheaper). In 1973 £200 million worth of development grants were made.

These grants can be treated in different ways, to increase or reduce pre-tax profits. They can be deducted from the cost of an asset when it is acquired, or they can be credited to the Profit and Loss Account. Whichever method is employed the result is the same in the end: the full benefit goes to the shareholders.

*Here is the Balance Sheet of a very simple company:*

| | | | |
|---|---|---|---|
| Share capital | £1000 | Buildings | £500 |
| | | Cash | £500 |
| | £1000 | | £1000 |

*Suppose the company spends £1000 on plant and equipment, for which it receives a £500 grant. If the company writes the value of the grant off the cost of the asset, the Balance Sheet will look like this.*

| | | | |
|---|---|---|---|
| Share Capital: £1000 | Buildings | | £500 |
| | Plant at cost | £1000 | |
| | Less investment | | |
| | grant of | £500 | |
| | | ——— | £500 |
| | | | ——— |
| | | | £1000 |

*If it is credited to the Profit and Loss Account, the Balance Sheet will look like this:*

| | | | |
|---|---|---|---|
| Share Capital: | £1000 | Buildings | £500 |
| Investment grant | | | |
| account: | £500 | Plant | £1000 |
| | ——— | | ——— |
| | £1500 | | £1500 |

Part of the £500 investment grant will be transferred to the Profit and Loss Account each year.

This is the impact that the different treatments have on the Profit and Loss Account of the company:

Suppose the company is making £3000 a year profit and depreciates the plant and equipment at 20 per cent on a straight line basis, i.e. 20 per cent of the cost is written off each year so that the equipment is written down to nothing in five years.

If the value of the investment grants has been written off the cost of the plant, the Profit and Loss Account will look like this:

| | |
|---|---|
| Profit | £3000 |
| Less depreciation | |
| (20% of £500) | £100 |
| | ——— |
| | £2900 |

*If the investment grant is kept as an item in the Balance Sheet and credited to the Profit and Loss Account over the life of the asset, the Profit and Loss Account will look like this:*

| | |
|---|---|
| Profit | £3000 |
| Depreciation | |
| (20% of £1000) | £200 |
| | ——— |
| Plus investment grant | |
| (one-fifth of £500) | £100 |
| | ——— |
| | £2900 |

*If the straight line depreciation policy is used, the write-offs and credits will always be equal and so the different way of treating grants will have no impact on the profits.*

**But:**

■ Profits will be reduced if the grant is credited to after-tax profits.

■ The system of crediting the grant to Profit and Loss over the life of the asset is the only system which will specifically show the value of the grant in the accounts.

To credit grants to pretax profits is the least conservative accounting treatment: it will tend to overstate profits. Investors tend to concentrate on a company's pretax profits when assessing the company's merits. Companies anxious to boost pretax profits will often employ accounting practices that overstate their profits relative to other companies.

**This is important to the worker: companies that overstate their profits in this way are likely to be less financially strong than they at first appear. This can reduce job security.**

■In 1973 Court Line, the shipping company, increased its pretax profits by £1,533,000 to £4.7 million by receiving a shipbuilding grant from the government.

The same accounts included several other accounting techniques that were much less conservative than those generally practised:

■Pretax profits were increased by including exceptional profits on the sale of shipbuilding contracts and investments and by taking credit for the results of several changes in accounting policy.

■Pretax profits were increased by excluding some operating costs. These were treated as additions to assets and credited to the Balance Sheet, rather than deducted from the Profit and Loss Account. This meant the cost was spread over a series of years – as the assets were depreciated, rather than concentrated in one year. These costs included advertising a Caribbean hotel, developing the company's computer, and interest paid on a loan to buy an aircraft.

■ In 1974 Court Line went bust.

**But:**

ICI credit investment grants below the line. (See the table on page 51).

In other companies, those £27.1 million worth of investment and regional grants would have been part of the pretax profit.

Companies that add investment grants to after-tax profits understate profits, compared to those companies which either deduct them from the cost of the asset or add them to pretax profits.

# Glossary and guide

## How to use this section:

This Glossary provides a way to understand the whole of the accounts of a company and a way to discover answers to specific problems such as: Is the company going bankrupt? Is the company likely to be taken over by an asset-stripper?

Technical terms and subjects are listed alphabetically with cross-references to those parts of the text in which they are explained.

The Glossary should be used together with the Index (page 197) which lists all terms used in the book.

### Asset-stripping:

The process of identifying and exploiting the concealed value or potential of a company's assets (normally property).

If an asset-stripper gains control of a company he may close a factory that can be profitably sold, or he may sell it and then continue to rent it, maintaining the established business. If the factory is closed – or moved to cheaper premises – there will be redundancies. This will be justified by saying that if the company were paying the **market rent** – instead of occupying the property for nothing – then its profits would be much lower. The asset-stripper will say that if the property were sold, the company could get a much higher return by investing the proceeds elsewhere. To keep the factory going is therefore a waste of resources. This means: to keep the factory going is not as profitable as selling it.

The asset-stripper is usually after property. You can find out if your employer is liable to be asset-stripped – either by the existing management or by being taken over – by discovering the value of the property and how recently it has been revalued (pages 136–138).

The company is more liable to be asset-stripped the higher the value of the property in relation to the **market capitalization** (see page 179) (in the case of public companies), or to profits (in the case of private companies).

Asset-stripping is a real threat to the workers even if the factory is kept open. (See pages 90–91).

### Auditors:

The auditors – almost always a firm of accountants – are appointed by the shareholders to produce the annual accounts. The confirmation of their appointment is a formality at the Annual General Meeting – in fact they are usually appointed by the directors.

### Bankruptcy:

A company is bankrupt when its liabilities (money the company owes) exceed its total assets (what it owns and is owed). When this happens the company is insolvent. The greater the difference between the company's total assets and its liabilities, the further away it is from bankruptcy. The total assets and liabilities can be worked out as follows.

**Total assets** = fixed assets (pages 136–139) + current assets (pages 142–144) — goodwill (pages 141–142) — research and development asset (pages 139–140).

**Goodwill** is not counted as an asset because it is intangible (page 141).

**Liabilities** = current liabilities (pages 145–147) + outside or long-term liabilities.

**Outside liabilities** = preference capital (page 121–122) + loan capital (page 126–127) + minority interests (page 131) + deferred liabilities (pages 132–136).

So in the Balance Sheet shown on page 118 the sum would work out:

|  | (figures in £000s) |
|---|---|
| Fixed assets | 48,969 |
| Current assets | 81,501 |
|  | ———— |
| Total assets | 129,570 |
| Current liabilities | 36,055 |
| Deferred liabilities | 5,515 |
| Preference capital | 5,880 |
| Minority interest | 2,035 |
| Loan capital | 21,551 |
|  | ———— |
|  | 71,036 |

So: Total assets
    less outside liabilities     58,534

This £58.5 million constitute the ordinary shareholders' funds: the value of the part of the business belonging to the shareholders. The company's solvency can be measured by expressing the ordinary shareholders' funds as a percentage of the total assets of the company. The higher the percentage the greater the company's solvency and the further it is away from bankruptcy. In the example given the **solvency ratio** is $\frac{58534}{129570} \times 100$, or 45 per cent.

**Remember:**

The assets in the Balance Sheet may be worth either more or less than the figures shown there. For example stocks may be overvalued (pages 142–43). Debtors may include some bad debts, thus overstating assets (page 144). Fixed assets may include undervalued freehold property (page 136).

The solvency ratio for British manufacturing industry as a whole is 45.5 per cent (source: **Financial Statistics**, November 1973, HMSO).

The solvency ratio can increase or decrease from year to year. The fact that the ratio is decreasing does not necessarily mean the business is contracting. An increase or a decrease can represent either an expansion or a contraction of the business.

If the expansion of the business is financed by retained profits or issuing more shares, then the assets will increase without increasing the outside liabilities. As a result the ratio will rise. But if fixed-interest capital is used to expand, the ratio will fall.

If a company is contracting, but can improve its liability position – by reducing the bank overdraft or paying its bills more quickly, the ratio might increase even though the company's business is falling, threatening job security.

**But:**

These sort of movements can happen only over a short time period. But if the company goes on losing money, the solvency ratio will fall.

**So:**

Use the solvency ratio as a guide to how soundly based the company is. If it has been falling over a long period of time, that means the company's position has been deteriorating. If it is very low but has remained unchanged, then the company is vulnerable to a sudden change for the worse. If the fall is a recent phenomenon, see if it is due to the way new expansion has been financed.

An important point is – a company can be insolvent and go bankrupt, even though it is potentially profitable. The need to buy large amounts of plant and materials before orders are delivered and paid for may mean that more money is leaving the business than is coming in, so that liabilities are continually mounting. Often it is a **liquidity crisis** – a shortage of ready cash – that causes the appointment of a **Receiver** and the closure of a business – even though the company is not insolvent and even though it is potentially profitable. (See pages 180–182.)

**Companies:**

**Holding:** See under parent.

**Parent:** This is the name given to the controlling company in a group of companies – it is sometimes called the holding company. It is the ultimate owner of the **subsidiary companies.** A typical structure for a company is:

Imperial Group

| Imperial Foods | John Player | St. Anne's Board Mill | Courage Ltd. |
|---|---|---|---|
| Ross Smedley Golden Foods  HP  Wonder Foods | | | John  Saccone  $33\frac{1}{2}$% Smith's & Speed  Harp (Tadcaster)  Lager |

This is a simplified family tree of the Imperial Group. The parent company – the ultimate holding company – is the Imperial Group, which has its shares quoted on the **Stock Exchange.** It has many **subsidiaries,** including the food division – Imperial Foods; the tobacco division – John Player; the brewery division – Courage; and the paper division – St Anne's Board Mills. Each of these divisions has subsidiaries of its own – Courage owns John Smith's Brewery, Tadcaster, a third of Harp Lager, and the wine merchant Saccone & Speed. These companies are subsidiaries of Courage, which is a subsidiary of Imperial Group. The Imperial Group is therefore called the **Parent Company** of all the companies in the group.

Although the Accounts of the subsidiaries may be useful in determining the size of the real profit the company is making, the Accounts of the parent company are a better guide. (See Chapter 5).

**Private:** See Chapter 12.

**Public:** See Chapter 12.

**Subsidiary:** A subsidiary company is a company that is owned by another company, its **parent company.**

**Nominee:** A nominee company is a company that acts as agent for a person or another company. Most commonly nominee companies are used to hold shares on behalf of someone. This means that when a shareholder is shown as a nominee company, it is virtually impossible to discover who the real owner of the shares is. Occasionally the shareholders of the nominee company – which can be established from Companies House – may give a clue to the identity of the people for whom the nominee company is acting.

### Directors:
The annual Report and Accounts will list the directors and details of directors' pay must be shown (page 93). If the directors appear to be paid very little, check on any other wealth they may own.

■ Do they have any shares in the company (pages 94–5)?

■ Do they have any other directorships (page 27)?

■ Did they start the company? If so, they will probably have become rich when the company became public. This information will come from the prospectus when the company was made public (page 36).

■ Do they receive valuable fringe benefits, like a house or car? (See pages 71–2.)

### Equity:
This is another name for the ordinary shares. Equity interest refers to that part of the business that belongs to the ordinary shareholders. It can be calculated from the Capital Employed side of the Balance Sheet (explained on pages 117, 120–136), by adding together the ordinary share capital, the reserves and any surplus on the revaluation of property that has not been incorporated in the accounts, less any goodwill (page 141) that appears on the other side of the Balance Sheet.

In the Balance Sheet shown on page 118 the value of the equity interest is £58,534,000. This is how much the shareholders would receive if the company was sold at its asset value, assuming the assets are not under- or over-valued.

The value of a company on the stock market (called the **market capitalization**) may often exceed this figure because share prices are related to the profitability and potential profitability of a company rather than its asset value. The market capitalization can be worked out by multiplying the price of the Company's shares (probably quoted in the *Financial Times*, see page 39) by the number of shares in issue (see pages 120–21).

In the case of private companies, making necessary provisions for the undervaluation of property, the value of equity interest is the best guide to the minimum value of a company. If it is a successful company, the goodwill of the business will be worth something in addition to the asset value.

### Investment:

How to tell how much the company has been investing.

The Notes to the Accounts will show changes in fixed assets – additions to and disposals of plant and machinery. Some companies publish a Source and Use of Funds table: this shows how much has been invested and where the money came from (page 53). Companies have to disclose their future intended spending. These are called **capital commitments.** When these have been authorized but not contracted for, it means the company has not yet signed the contracts for the work: such decisions can easily be reversed if necessary.

Have companies been investing abroad? Companies are not obliged to say where any money has been spent, though some do. Nor are they required to show the overseas labour force, though if they do, it can be a clue to expansion abroad.

### Liquidity:

A company's liquidity is its ability to pay its bills. A liquid asset is one that can be turned into cash within a year. If a company's current assets (pages 142–44) exceed its current liabilities (pages 145–47) then it is said to be liquid. This means that it can pay its bills and carry on its business without difficulties. The extent of a company's liquidity can be measured by the **liquidity** or **current ratio,** which is the ratio of current assets to current liabilities. It is worked out as follows:

$$\frac{\text{Current assets}}{\text{Current liabilities}} : 1$$

In the example of the Balance Sheet on page 118 the liquidity ratio is 2.26:1. This means that for every £ the company owes it has £2.26 owed to it. The higher the ratio, the greater the company's liquidity. Companies with high liquidity are in a strong position during credit squeezes – when bank money is short. But the liquidity ratio is not always an accurate guide to the company's ability to pay its bills because current assets cannot always be turned into cash easily.

The most common current asset is stocks. So there is a second ratio used to judge the company's liquidity: the **quick ratio.** This is worked out as follows:

$$\frac{\text{Quick assets}}{\text{Current liabilities}} : 1$$

Quick assets are the current assets minus stocks and work in progress. In the example on page 118 the quick assets are (in £000s) $81,501 - 47,321 = 34,180$.

$$\text{So the quick ratio is } \frac{34,180}{36,055} : 1 = 0.95:1$$

The average liquidity ratio for UK manufacturing industry is: 1.72:1.

The average quick ratio is: 1.03:1.

These ratios are useful to workers as signposts to the way in which the company is managed and to the security of their jobs. The lower these ratios the more vulnerable the company is to its suppliers and the bank – the main headings under current liabilities. The company may encounter problems if trading conditions get difficult and suppliers press to be paid or the bank asks for its money back. As long as the company as a whole is solvent (see Bankruptcy above), and providing there are easily realizable fixed assets which can be sold or used as security for borrowing the liquidity problem can be overcome. But a company with liquidity problems may start selling property to raise money to improve its current asset position, or it may close down an activity that is not very profitable but which ties up a lot of assets.

If the liquidity ratio is very high this may mean:
■ The company is carrying too high a level of stocks.
■ The company is not collecting money owed to it quickly. (The length of time a company allows its debtors to pay can be worked out using the explanation on page 144).
■ The company is keeping a high proportion of assets in current assets, that could be used more usefully elsewhere.

If the ratios show a sharp decrease from one year to the next (i.e. liabilities rise relative to assets) this could mean the company is having to borrow money or delay paying bills.

If the company is expanding production, the stock figure may increase but as the stocks have been financed from either overdrafts or trade creditors, there will probably be no change in the ratios.

**But if the ratios show a continuing decline over a period of years it probably means that the company is heading for a liquidity crisis.**

### Market rent:
The rent that could be obtained for property if it were let at today's prices. A lot of companies lease property on terms agreed years ago, so the rent today is well below the market rent.

### Profits:
**Past** – in the case of public companies, these are obtainable from Extel statistical cards (page 34) and annual accounts (page 33). Some public companies have a table of profits over the years in the accounts.

For private companies the profit record can be established from the accounts, which are in Companies House (page 27).

**Present:** from the Profit and Loss Account (page 44).

**Future:** It is impossible to forecast future profits from the Balance Sheet alone because they depend on many factors including the company's competitive position and demand for its product. Profits are likely to increase for one of three reasons:

■ An increase in sales.
■ An increase in prices.
■ The result of management moves to increase the return on the company's assets. This could involve redundancies, factory closures and changes in the use of assets.

Increases in prices and the volume of sales may be referred to in the Chairman's statement (page 96). Companies have no statutory obligation to disclose the size of their order book. There may be clues in the Balance Sheet – has there been a build-up of stocks, ready for sale?

Changes in the use of the assets will also generally be referred to in the Chairman's statement. Have profits been exceptionally depressed by reorganization (page 55)? Has there been an improvement in the company's liquidity? Has there been a change in the company's fixed assets, representing new investment (page 89)?

### Profitability:

**Measuring profitability:** There are two ways in which profitability can be measured:

- The profits made from the company's sales.
- The profits made from the company's assets.

The profit made from the company's sales is called the **profit margin.** The profit made from the company's assets is called the **return on capital employed.**

If a company's sales are £1000 and its profits £100, then the profit margin is 10 per cent. $(\frac{£100 \times 100\%}{£1000})$.

But arguments that companies are very unprofitable because they have low margins should be distrusted. They ignore the return on capital and the risk – or lack of it – in volved.

During 1973–74 most major retailers bemoaned the fact that margins were low. They did not say what the return on capital was.

In 1973 Tesco's pre-tax profit was £21,727,000. Its sales were £359 million. So the pre-tax margin was 6.05 per cent – or 6p in every £ you spent there.
But: The company's assets were £57 million. So the return on capital was 45.8 per cent.

This means that for every £ spent on buildings, shop fittings etc, Tesco made 45.8p profit. If you put your money in the building society, you will get about 10p for every £ you invest.

There is little risk in retailing. The goods are sold for cash, but the suppliers have to wait for their money. Tesco's Balance Sheet shows that it was owed around £3 million, but that it owed its suppliers £35.5 million.

When companies claim they are not profitable, look at both the margin and return on capital ratio. Work out the profit per worker: Tesco's total wage bill is only £8 million more than its pre-tax profits.

### Stock Exchange:

The Stock Exchange is the building which houses the **Stock Market,** where shares are bought and sold. **Stockbrokers** advise investors which shares to buy, and carry out the business for them. **Jobbers** stand in the Stock Market and match the buyers and sellers. The Stock Exchange is chiefly a market place in which second hand assets – shares of companies – can change hands. It is of hardly any importance in raising new money to invest in industry: less than 1 per cent in 1973. When someone buys a share, they buy the right to a share of the company's profits – the share already exists and the money does not go to the company. Of course, originally the company did receive money from the original subscriber for the shares.

# Appendix 1

**Where to find Extel cards:**

B (Full British Service)
U (Unquoted Service)

**Aberdeen:**
Aberdeen Central Library (B & U)
      Rosemount Viaduct, Aberdeen AB9 1GU

**Aylesbury:**
Buckinghamshire County Library (B)
      Walton Street, Aylesbury HP20 1UU

**Bedford:**
Bedford Central Library (B)
      Harpur Street, Bedford MK40 1PG

**Belfast:**
Belfast Central Library (B & U)
      Royal Avenue, Belfast BT1 1EA

**Berkhamsted:**
Ashridge Management College (B & U)
      Berkhamsted, Herts.

**Birmingham:**
Birmingham Reference Library (B & U)
      Birmingham B1 2AR
Commerce Central Library (B)
      Aston Street, Birmingham B4 74A

**Blackburn:**
Blackburn Central Library (B & U)
      Library Street, Blackburn BB1 7AJ

**Bradford:**
Bradford Central Library (U)
      Princes Way, Bradford BD1 1NN

**Camberley:**
Business Education & Training Service (B & U)
    26 Sheriden Road, Frimley, Camberley, Surrey

**Canterbury:**
University of Kent Library (B)
    Canterbury

**Chelmsford:**
Anglian Regional Management Centre (B & U)
    Danbury Park, Danbury, Chelmsford CM3 4AT
Essex County Library (B & U)
    Goldlay Gardens, Chelmsford CM2 0EW

**Cranfield:**
Cranfield Institute of Technology (B & U)
    Cranfield, Bedfordshire

**Cheltenham:**
Cheltenham Division Library (B)
    Clarence Street, Cheltenham, Gloucestershire GL50 3JT

**Coventry:**
University of Warwick (B & U)
    Coventry CV4 7AL

**Dudley:**
Dudley Central Library (B)
    St. James's Road, Dudley DY1 1HR

**Dundee:**
Dundee Central Library (B)
    Albert Square, Dundee DD1 1DB

**Edinburgh:**
Edinburgh Central Library (B & U)
    George IV Bridge, Edinburgh EH1 1EG
Heriot-Watt University (B)
    Mountbatten Building, 31–35 Grassmarket,
    Edinburgh EH1 2HT
Napier College of Science & Technology (B)
    Colinton Road, Edinburgh EH10 5DT

**Exeter:**

University of Exeter (B)
>Department of Economics, Streatham Court,
>Rennes Drive, Exeter

**Glasgow:**

Glasgow Public Libraries (B & U)
>Commercial Library, Royal Exchange Square,
>Glasgow C1

**Huddersfield:**

Huddersfield Polytechnic (B & U)
>Queensgate, Huddersfield HD1 3DH

**Hull:**

Kingston upon Hull Central Library (U)
>Albion Street, Kingston upon Hull

Hull College of Commerce (B)
>Queens Gardens, Kingston upon Hull HU1 3DH

**Kingston upon Thames:**

Kingston Polytechnic Library (B)
>Penrhyn Road, Kingston upon Thames KT1 2EE

**Leeds:**

Leeds Polytechnic (B & U)
>Business & Social Sciences Library,
>Calverley Street, Leeds LS1 3HL

**Leicester:**

Leicester Central Library (B & U)
>Bishop Street, Leicester LE1 6AA

**Liverpool:**

Liverpool Public Libraries (B & U)
>William Brown Street, Liverpool L3 8EW

Liverpool Polytechnic Faculty of Engineering and Science
Library (B)
>Byrom Street, Liverpool L3 3AF

Liverpool University (B)
>11 Abercromby Square, Liverpool L69 3BX

**London:**
City Business Library (U)
    Gillett House, 55 Basinghall Street, London EC2 5BX
City University Graduate Business Centre (B & U)
    23 Goswell Road, London EC1
Commercial and Technical Reference Library (U)
    Acton Library, High Street, London W3 6NA
Holborn Reference Library (B & U)
    32–38 Theobalds Road, London WC1X 8PA
London Graduate School of Business Studies (B & U)
    Sussex Place, Regent's Park, London NW1 4SA

**Loughborough:**
Loughborough University of Technology (B & U)
    Loughborough, Leicestershire

**Manchester:**
Manchester Business School (B & U)
    Booth Street West, Manchester M15 6PB
Manchester Central Library (B & U)
    St Peters Square, Manchester M2 5PD

**Newcastle upon Tyne:**
Newcastle upon Tyne Central Library (B & U)
    Princess Square, Newcastle upon Tyne NE99 1MC
Newcastle upon Tyne Polytechnic (B & U)
    Ellison Building, Ellison Place,
    Newcastle upon Tyne NE1 8ST

**North Shields:**
North Tyneside Central Library (B & U)
    Howard Street, North Shields NE30 1LY

**Norwich:**
Norwich Central Library (B)
    Bethel Street, Norwich NOR 57E

**Oxford:**
St Catherine's College (B)
    Oxford OX1 3UJ

**Paisley:**
Paisley College of Technology (B)
High Street, Paisley, Renfrewshire

**Salford:**
University of Salford Library (B & U)
Salford M5 4WT

**Sheffield:**
Sheffield Central Library (U)
Surrey Street, Sheffield S1 1XZ
Sheffield Polytechnic (B)
Department of Accountancy &
Professional Studies, Pond Street
Sheffield S1 1WB

**Shrewsbury:**
Shropshire County Library (U)
Column House, 7 London Road
Shrewsbury ST2 6NW

**Slough:**
Slough College of Technology (B)
Williams Street, Slough

**Stevenage:**
Hertfordshire County Library (B & U)
Central Library, Southgate, Stevenage, SG1 1HD

**Stockport:**
Stockport Central Library (U)
Wellington Road South, Stockport SK1 3RS

**Sunderland:**
Sunderland Polytechnic (B & U)
Chester Street, Sunderland, Co. Durham

**Winchester:**
Hampshire County Library (B)
North Walls, Winchester

**Wolverhampton:**
Wolverhampton Polytechnic (B)
Wolverhampton WV1 1LY

# Appendix 2:

### Summary of Disclosure Requirements under the Companies Acts 1948–1967

Source: *Guide to the Accounting Requirements of the Companies Acts 1948–1967* published for the General Education Trust of the Institute of Chartered Accountants in England and Wales by Gee & Co. (Publishers) Ltd.

1. Every limited company whether public or private is required to file, with its annual return, a certified copy of its balance sheet (including profit and loss account and other annexures), and certified copies of the auditors' report and director's report.

2. The following particulars are required to be shown:

### Balance sheet:

i. Authorised and issued share capital, summarised.

ii. Redeemable preference shares.

iii. Shares in company held by subsidiaries or their nominees.

iv. Options on unissued shares.

v. Arrears of fixed cumulative dividends.

vi. Share capital on which interest has been paid out of capital.

vii. Reserves – aggregate amount and under headings appropriate to the company's business.

viii. Capital redemption reserve fund.

ix. Share premium account.

x. Movement on reserves.

xi. Liabilities and provisions.

xii. Debentures of the company held for the company by nominee or trustee.

xiii. Debentures of company held by subsidiaries.

xiv. Redeemed debentures which may be re-issued.

xv. Liabilities secured on assets of the company.

xvi. Particulars of any charge on the assets of the company.

xvii. Amounts set aside for the purpose of meeting undue fluctuations in charges for taxation.

xviii. Movements on provisions, i.e. amounts written off or retained to provide for depreciation, renewals or diminution in value of assets; or amounts retained to provide for any known liability which cannot be determined with substantial accuracy.

xix. Aggregate amount of bank loans and overdrafts.

xx. Aggregate amount of other borrowings, repayable wholly or in part more than five years from date of balance sheet, and details of terms of borrowing.

xxi. Basis on which any amount set aside for UK corporation tax is computed.

xxii. Amounts of inter-group indebtedness.

xxiii. Gross recommended dividend.

xxiv. Contingent liabilities.

xxv. Future capital expenditure.

xxvi. Assets – under headings appropriate to the business. Fixed assets, current assets and other assets to be separately identified.

xxvii. Methods used to arrive at amount of fixed assets under each heading.

xxviii. Normal method for each fixed assets, cost or valuation plus aggregate amount provided or written off for depreciation and difference between these amounts.

xxix. Fixed assets included at a valuation.

xxx. Movement on fixed assets (other than investment).

xxxi. Land held as fixed assets.

xxxii. Goodwill, patents and trade-marks.

xxxiii. Quoted investments and unquoted investments in equity share capital.

xxxiv. Shares in and aggregate amounts owing from subsidiaries.

xxxv. Shares in fellow subsidiaries, in aggregate.

xxxvi. Other group indebtedness.

xxxvii. Current assets.

xxxviii. Loans to employees or officers of the company.

xxxix. Manner in which stock in trade or work in progress is computed.

xl. Certain expenditure incurred on any issue of share capital or debentures or in connection with shares or debentures.

xli. Basis of conversion of foreign currencies.

xlii. Corresponding amounts for the preceding financial year.

### Profit and loss account:

i. Turnover and method by which it is arrived at. Exemptions are given to banking or discounting companies, or to companies not being holding or subsidiary companies where the turnover is less than £50,000.

ii. Incomes from rents of land – if a substantial part of company's revenue.

iii. Income from investments, distinguishing between income from quoted and unquoted investments.

iv. Directors' emoluments.

v. Chairman's emoluments.

vi. Emoluments of employees receiving more than £10,000 per annum. The number of employees whose emoluments fall in each bracket or a scale in multiples of £2,500 starting at £10,000.

vii. Auditor's remuneration.

viii. Interest payable – on bank loans, overdrafts and loans repayable within five years and on all other loans.

ix. Amounts charged to revenue for hire of plant and machinery, if material.

x. Provision for depreciation.

xi. Method of calculation of depreciation, if other than by reference to amount of assets.

xii. Taxation – UK corporation tax (and basis of computation); UK income tax (and basis of computation); overseas tax.

xiii. Amounts provided respectively for redemption of share capital and loans.

xiv. Transfers or proposed transfers to or from reserves and provisions.

xv. Aggregate amount of dividends paid and proposed.

xvi. Charges and credits relating to prior years.

xvii. Factors materially affecting items shown in the profit and loss account.

xviii. Corresponding amounts for the preceding financial year.

**Directors' report:**

**i.** Corresponding amounts of the preceding financial year.

**ii.** Recommended dividend.

**iii.** Proposed transfers to reserves.

**iv.** Directors' names.

**v.** Principal activities of company and its subsidiaries, including any significant changes.

**vi.** Significant changes in fixed assets of company. Banking, discount, insurance and shipping companies are exempted.

**vii.** Where market value of land held as fixed assets is substantially different from book amount, the difference must be stated. Exemptions as in (vi) above.

**viii.** Issues of shares or debentures during financial year.

**ix.** Any interest of director in contract with the company.

**x.** Directors' rights to acquire shares or debentures and directors' interests in shares or debentures of the company.

**xi.** Analysis of turnover and profit or loss before taxation of the company or group between substantially different classes of business, showing the proportions in which turnover is divided amongst those classes, and the extent to which each class of business has contributed to, or restricted, the profit or loss of the company.

**xii.** Average number of employees per week, if one hundred or more.

**xiii.** Aggregate remuneration paid or payable to employees for year, if one hundred or more.

**xiv.** Political and charitable contributions made by the company or group showing separate totals of each if they exceed £50 in total.

**xv.** Value of goods exported, if total turnover exceeds £50,000. Certain companies are exempted from disclosing turnover where the Department of Industry agree that disclosure would be harmful to the national interest.

*Certain additional information to be given in accounts*

**i.** Identity of holding company.

**ii.** Investments in subsidiaries and other companies.

## Disclosure Requirements under the Rules and Regulations of the Stock Exchange

The rules quoted are those of the London Stock Exchange, which are also applied to other stock exchanges in Great Britain.

**1.** To comply with the requirements of the Council of the Stock Exchange, London, quoted companies have to give a general undertaking to the Council. The undertaking details the information required to be supplied to the Quotations Department. Under the requirements companies must notify the Quotations Department without delay the date of the board meeting at which the declaration or recommendation of a dividend will be considered, or at which any announcement of the profits or losses in respect of any financial period or part thereof will be approved for publication, and must notify the Quotations Department by the quickest possible means immediately after the relevant board meeting of:

i. all dividends or cash bonuses recommended;

ii. the preliminary profits announcements for the year or half year;

iii. short particulars of any proposed issue of shares or other securities.


**2.** Companies must also notify without delay:

i. particulars of any acquisitions or realisations of assets;

ii. any information required to be disclosed to the Stock Exchange under the provisions of the City Code on Takeovers and Mergers;

iii. any changes in the directors;

iv. any proposed change in the general character or nature of the business or any change in voting control or in beneficial ownership of the securities carrying voting control;

v. intention to make a drawing of any redeemable securities with the amount and date;

vi. amount of securities outstanding after a drawing has been made;

vii. any other information necessary to enable the shareholders to appraise the position of the company and to avoid the establishment of a false market in the securities.

**3.** Companies must also forward to the Quotations Department:

**i.** proofs for approval of all circulars to holders of securities, notices of meetings (other than routine annual general meetings), forms of proxy and notices by advertisement to holders of bearer securities;

**ii.** all circulars, notices, reports or other documents at the same time as they are issued to holders of securities.

**iii.** all resolutions passed declaring dividends, re-electing directors and auditors.

**4.** The following minimum information should be circularised to the holders of securities, when preliminary announcements in respect of any year, half-year or other accounting period or part thereof are made in relation to:

**A holding company:**

**i.** group profit (or loss) after all charges including taxation;

**ii.** U.K. and, where material, overseas taxation charged in arriving at (i) above;

**iii.** amount of group profit (or loss) attributable to members of holding company;

**iv.** if material, the extent to which group profit has been affected by special credits (e.g. from transfer from reserves, etc.) and/or debits;

**v.** rates of dividends of holding company paid and proposed and the amount absorbed thereby;

**vi.** comparative figures of i to v above in respect of corresponding previous period;

**vii.** any supplementary information which in the opinion of the directors is necessary for a reasonable appreciation of the results or other material changes in the aggregate of the balance or profit and loss account and other reserves of the group.

**A company not a holding company:**
Similar information to that listed above must be submitted.

**5.** Quoted companies must include in or circulate with annual reports:

i. *a.* a description of the operations carried on by the company or group;

   *b.* if the company or group carries on widely differing operations, a statement showing the contributions from these and the trading results;

   *c.* if the company or group trades outside the United Kingdom, a statement showing a geographical analysis of its trading operations.

ii. If the company has subsidiaries:

   *a.* their names and countries of operation;

   *b.* the percentage of its equity capital attributable to the company's interest.

iii. If the company or group has interests in associated companies, then similar information to that in **ii** above should be given, together with particulars of issued share and loan capital and the total amount of reserves.

iv. A statement showing the beneficial interest of persons and directors in the share capital of the company, and the amount of the holdings.

v. Particulars if any director(s) has agreed to waive his emoluments.

**6.** Quoted companies must open for inspection from the date of notice of the annual general meeting until the annual general meeting takes place:

i. a statement of all transactions of each director;

ii. copies of all contracts of service for any director of the company. Companies must notify all shareholders and debenture-holders that these are available for inspection.

# Index